THE BEAUTIES … T

COUNTIE…

An attempt to depict the ancient counties of Wales &
Illustrated with 18th and 19th century engravings
Compiled by

David S. Yerburgh

2008

Bangor, Caernarfonshire

Drawn by T. Compton & aquatinted by D. Havell

1816

Published by
Revd. Canon David Yerburgh,
2, Mill Race Close, Salisbury SP2 7RX

Printed by
The Baskerville Press
6-8 Newton Road, Salisbury SP2 7QA

ISBN 978 0 9535635 8 6

PREFACE

THE ANCIENT COUNTIES OF WALES

CAMBRIA

On SCENES like these the eye delights to dwell;
Here loud CASCADES - and there the silent DELL,
MOUNTAINS of towering height - fantastic shape,
At whose broad base, terrific CHASMS gape:
HILLS, clothed in gayest verdure, smile serene,
Whilst rude and barren ROCKS, contrast the scene.
Varied by light and shade's perpetual change,
The enraptured ARTIST finds an endless range.

These are the words of introduction to the well known book 'Wales Illustrated in a Series of Views', a book of one hundred and sixty eight views of Wales, engraved on steel from original drawings by Henry Gastineau, c.1830. They also satisfactorily sum up in a few words the purpose of this present volume.

This book has been designed to try to describe something of the diversity of the scenery, the places and the objects of interest that are to be found so abundantly in the thirteen ancient counties of Wales. These varied aspects of God's and man's creation, are illustrated by the skills of a variety of eighteenth and nineteenth century artists and engravers.

David S. Yerburgh, Salisbury 2008

INTRODUCTION

In 1997 I was asked by the National Library of Wales to help put on an exhibition of engravings that depicted the many superb waterfalls in Wales. After the exhibition was over I decided to publish a small book, which I entitled *'A Tour of the Waterfalls of Wales'*. It was the success of both the exhibition and the sale of the book that prompted me to look to other avenues of the engravers skill.

This interest in engravings was further encouraged when the National Library of Wales, as part of their celebration of the Millennium asked me to assist with another exhibition of engravings depicting *'The Abbeys, Priories and Cathedrals of Wales'*. It was in preparation for this exhibition that I wrote my second book as a guide to the exhibition in 2000.

In my research for these two exhibitions I soon discovered that the National Library possessed many rare topographical books of engravings. These books skilfully illustrate many of the varied scenes of Wales, using different mediums of engraving. This discovery quickly prompted me to write three more books based on three of the books that I had seen in the library.

The first of these three books was a book on the former 18th century estate of Hafod, made famous by the book written by Elisabeth Inglis entitled *'Peacocks in Paradise'*. My guide for my book was the large volume entitled *'A Tour of Hafod'* by J.E. Smith and illustrated with fifteen superb coloured aquatints by J. Stadler. The second of these books was based on a delightful small volume written, engraved and hand coloured by William Weston Young in 1835, entitled *'The Beauties of Glyn Neath'*, which gives a splendid picture of the waterfalls, houses and topography of the area covered today by the Vale of Neath. My last book, in this series of three, was based upon a delightful book of coloured aquatints by Thomas

Compton, entitled *'The Northern Cambrian Mountains'*, written in 1817. I used this book as a guide to the Snowdonia National Park under the title *'An attempt to depict the Northern Cambrian Mountains or the Snowdonia National Park'*.

Having written one book on the Snowdonia National Park I then felt that I should try and produce a similar book for *'The Brecon Beacons National Park'*. However, unlike Snowdonia, I couldn't find any book that covered the whole area in one illustrated book. So this particular book included a variety of 18th and 19th century engravings and a number of black and white photographs to fill some gaps where I couldn't find any engraving.

My next book was different from the rest in this series so far in that it described and illustrated a series of *'Tours from the town of Llangollen'*, the annual home of the International Music Eisteddfod. This book was mainly based upon the many attractions that can be found in the former old counties of Denbighshire and Flintshire.

In 2006 I finally, after many years of research, put together a book, which was designed to give an artistic impression of *'The Castles in Wales that were built by the former Welsh Princes'*, rather than by the English. Again, like the Brecon book, the number of engravings available was very limited and I had to rely on black and white photographic images for many of the lesser sites.

Having written books on the two National parks based on Snowdon and Brecon I felt that I should complete the trilogy by producing one more book based upon *'The Pembrokeshire Coast National Park'*. This was printed in 2007 and is different from the rest of my other books in that the engraving and the text appear together on one page rather than on two. At the end of each section there is list of other places of interest, but without any engravings to match them.

So I come to this current and final book on Wales, which I have entitled *'An attempt to depict the beauties of the ancient counties of Wales'* with the sub heading, *'An artistic impression of the ancient counties of Wales, based upon 18th & 19th century engravings'*. In this book I have taken the six old counties of North Wales and the six old counties of South Wales (plus the county of Monmouthshire, which under the old counties was part of England but today is part of Wales.) I then chose a number of engravings from each of these thirteen counties in an attempt to give an overall picture of the whole of Wales in a series of engravings. Occasionally it has proved difficult to find any suitable engraving for certain views, so I have included a few original drawings by artists, who were contemporary with the engravings and who are well known for their painting of Welsh topography.

One of the problems that have arisen is what engravings to include and what ones to leave out, as some counties like Caernarfonshire and Merionethshire have so many engravings and sites to choose from, whereas Montgomeryshire and Radnorshire have far less. However, I felt that I should treat each county the same and so I have limited each county to just ten engravings. In this way one can get an over all picture of the whole of ancient counties of Wales and hence the title *'An attempt to depict the beauties of the ancient counties of Wales, an artistic impression.'*

THE BEAUTIES OF THE ANCIENT COUNTIES OF WALES

NORTH WALES

SOUTH WALES

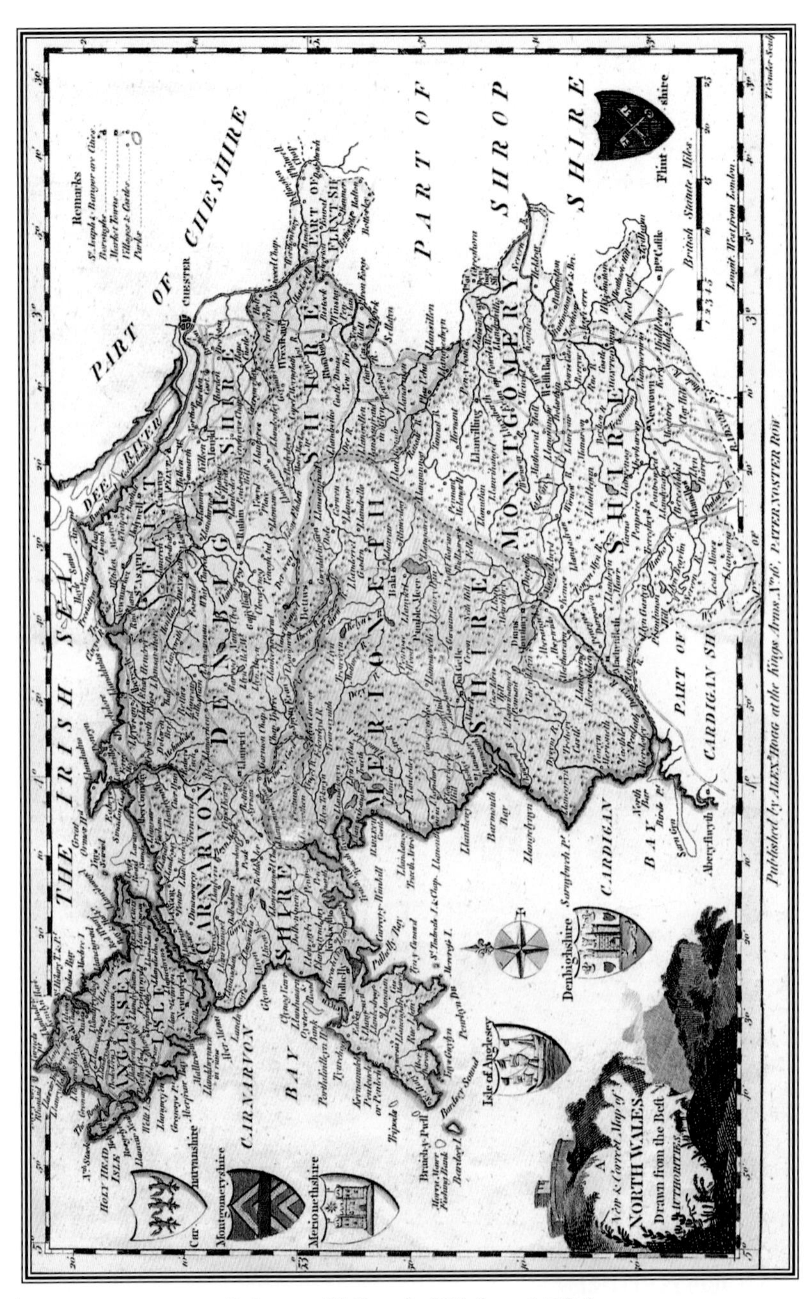

Map of North Wales 1794

THE SIX ANCIENT COUNTIES OF NORTH WALES

1. ANGLESEY

2. CAERNARFONSHIRE

3. DENBIGHSHIRE

4. FLINTSHIRE

5. MERIONETHSHIRE

6. MONTGOMERYSHIRE

THE ANCIENT COUNTY OF ANGLESEY

The Menai Bridge
(Frontispiece to North Wales Illustrated)

Drawn by H. Gastineau & engraved by T.Barber

1830

THE ANCIENT COUNTY OF ANGLESEY

1. Beaumaris Bay

2. Beaumaris Castle

3. Holyhead

4. Holyhead, the rocks

5. Llanfair P G, Marquess of Anglesey's Column

6. Menai Bridge

7. Penmon Priory, Dovecote & Well

8. Plas Newydd, the Great Cromlech

9. Skerries Lighthouse

10. South Stack

ANGLESEY 1

BEAUMARIS BAY

OS 125 : 607 760

Having crossed the Menai Strait by the famous Menai Bridge, built by Thomas Telford in 1819-26, one comes, after four miles, to the charming seaside resort of Beaumaris. This small town is dominated be the perfectly proportioned Beaumaris castle (see the next page). Thomas Compton must have drawn the original drawing for the aquatint below of Beaumaris Bay just about the same time as Thomas Telford began to build his bridge across the Strait. The crossing up to that time would have to have been by boat, as in the picture.

Beaumaris Bay

Drawn by T. Compton & engraved by D. Havell

1816

ANGLESEY 2

BEAUMARIS CASTLE

OS 115 : 606 763

Beaumaris Castle is a concentric castle of almost perfect symmetry and is encircled by a once tidal moat. It was the last of Edward I Welsh castles to be built and was designed by the architect James of St George. Although the castle was never completed it was declared to be in a state of defence by 1298. Beaumaris Castle is particularly noted for its sophisticated defences, which in the event were virtually never used. The inner wall, with its towers, is well known for its continuous internal passage. The castle is now in the care of Cadw and is open to the public.

Beaumaris Castle

Drawn & etched by J.G. Wood

1813

ANGLESEY 3

HOLYHEAD

OS 114 : 247 827

Holyhead was in origin a Roman fort (Caer Gybi) and the home of a Celtic Christian settlement, but is now a commercial and industrial town with a busy harbour regularly taking boats to Ireland. Holyhead also marks the end of Telford's road through Snowdonia, across the Menai Bridge to Holyhead Harbour. The church of St Cybi is a reminder of the 6th century saint who founded a Christian community here. The present church is mainly 15-17th century, with a 13th century choir.

Holyhead Church & Harbour

Drawn & engraved on wood by H. Hughes

1823

ANGLESEY 4

HOLYHEAD, THE ROCKS

OS 114 : 215 841

Edward Pugh in his book Cambria Depicta (1816) gives a vivid description of the caves which can be seen near Holyhead. 'The different mouths of these caves form pictures by themselves. Part of this rock shoots up perpendicularly from the sea to the amazing height of the hill above and gives completely the idea of the vast square tower of a cathedral, in the Gothic style. The mind, which is impressed with religious ideas, cannot contemplate this piece of natural curiosity without the feelings of awe and admiration of the Author of all nature.'

Cavernous Rocks near Holyhead

Drawn by E. Pugh & aquatinted by J. Havell

1813

ANGLESEY 5

Nr LLANFAIR PWLLGWYNGYLL, THE COLUMN

OS 115 : 535 716

The Marquess of Anglesey's 90 foot column was erected in 1817 to commemorate the distinguished military service of the first marquess, who commanded the cavalry at the Battle of Waterloo, and where he lost a leg. The statue on the top of the column (not shown in the Print) was added in 1860. The column stand on Craig y Dinas, 170 feet above sea level, where it commands a splendid view over the Menai Strait to CAERNARFONSHIRE and to Plas Newydd, the home of the present marquess and now in the care of the National trust.

The Marquess of Anglesey's Column

Drawn & engraved on wood by H. Hughes

1823

ANGLESEY 6
THE MENAI BRIDGE

OS 115 : 556 715

Until 1826 the only access into Anglesey was by boat (see p.10). However, between 1819-1826, Thomas Telford was busily engaged in building the famous 1000ft Menai Suspension Bridge at a 100 feet above the sea, in order to allow the tall ships to pass safely below the bridge. The bridge was considerably rebuilt between 1938-1941, when the bridge was widened and strengthened. A mile southwest is Robert Stephenson's Britannia Bridge which was originally a tubular rail bridge, until it was rebuilt as a conventional rail and road bridge in 1972.

The Menai Bridge

Drawn by D. Cox & engraved by W. Ratclyffe

1836

ANGLESEY 7

PENMON PRIORY

OS 115 : 630 808

St Seriol originally founded Penmon Priory in the 6th century and the church was rebuilt between 1120-1170. In 1237 Llewelyn ap Gruffydd granted the monastery and its property to the prior and canons of Priestholm (Puffin Island) who then moved to Penmon and reorganized the community as Austin Canons. The church and the domestic buildings are now separate, the former serving as a parish church, and the latter is in the care of Cadw. The stone roofed dovecote was built shortly before the monastery was dissolved. Close by is St Seriol's Well, which may well mark the site of St Seriol's 6th century monastery.

Penmon Priory near Beaumaris

Coloured lithograph, artist & lithographer not known.

c. 1850

By kind permission of Llyfrgell Genedlaethol Cymru / The National Library of Wales.

ANGLESEY 8

PLAS NEWYDD

OS 115 : 521 698

Plas Newydd is the magnificent, mainly 18th century, mansion of the Marquess of Anglesey, but is now in the care of the National Trust. As well as the many splendid pieces or furniture and portraits it also has an important collection of works by Rex Whistler and his largest and last trompe l'oeil mural, in the renaissance style. Behind the house stands a vast double cromlech, which the largest stone is 23ft long, 12ft broad and four ft thick supported by five stones. The second is similar in construction but much smaller. This is just one of many ancient burial sites in Anglesey.

Great Cromlech at Plas Newydd

Drawn & etched by J.G. Wood

1813

ANGLESEY 9

SKERRIES LIGHTHOUSE

OS 114 : 268 952

The Skerries lighthouse, with a ridge of rocks called the Cardinals, can best be seen two miles north west of Carmel Head. The first lighthouse to be built on Skerries was in 1730 when it cost £3,000. This first lighthouse was lit by coal in a grate at the cost of £150 a year, however this expenditure was quickly recouped by the toll imposed on all the vessels that passed the lighthouse. It was rebuilt in 1804 when the coal lighting was replaced by oil lighting and the toll was discontinued.

The Skerries Lighthouse

Drawn by E. Pugh & aquatinted by J. Havell

1813

ANGLESEY 10

SOUTH STACK

OS 114 : 203 824

South Stack is a small island, which nestles just below the steep Cliff of Holyhead Mountain the highest point in Anglesey (720ft). The sixty foot lighthouse was built in 1809 has a revolving light as opposed to the Skerries lighthouse, which when it was built was stationary. On the approach to South Stack there is some spectacular cliff scenery, ancient remains, hut circles and a RSPB observation post. From the parking place there are steps and a narrow bridge leading to the lighthouse.

South Stack Lighthouse

Drawn & engraved on wood by H. Hughes

1823

THE ANCIENT COUNTY OF CAERNARFONSHIRE

Aberglaslyn

Drawn by T.Compton & aquatinted by T.Cartwright

1816

THE ANCIENT COUNTY OF CAERNARFONSHIRE

1. Bangor Cathedral, Penrhyn Castle, Aber Falls

2. Beddgelert & Aberglaslyn

3. Criccieth, Llyn Peninsula, Portmerion, & Portmadog

4. Caernarfon & Conwy Castles

5. Betws Y.Coed, Swallow, Conwy & Machno Falls

6. Llanberis, Dolbadarn & Ceunant Mawr

7. Dolwyddelan Castle

8. Llyn Gwyant, Nant Lle & Llyn Dinas

9. Nant Ffrancon, Ogwen Bank & Ogwen Falls

10. Snowdon Mountain

CAERNARFONSHIRE 1

BANGOR CATHEDRAL

OS 115 : 581 721

The engraving below depicts Bangor cathedral in the early 19th century and it looks much the same on the outside today as it did then. The cathedral is the oldest cathedral that has been in continuous use in Great Britain. St Dieniol, who became Bishop of Bangor in 546, founded a monastery in Bangor in 525. The fabric of the cathedral has suffered from invaders and from native rebels and has undergone frequent repair and there are only a few remains of the original Norman church. In 1868 Sir Gilbert Scott began a major restoration programme which took six years to complete. Close to Bangor can be seen massive Penrhyn Castle built between 1820-1840 (OS : 115 605 720) and the impressive Aber Falls.(OS : 115 668 699).

Bangor Cathedral

Drawn by H. Gastineau & engraved by W. Wallis

1830

CAERNARFONSHIRE 2
BEDDGELERT & PONT ABERGLASLYN

OS 115 : 593 483 & 594 464

Beddgelert, 'The Grave of Gelert'. was named after Gelert, the trusted hound of Prince Llewelyn who had left him in charge of his son, while he went hunting. On his return he found the boy missing and his hound with blood stains on his mouth. Llewelyn, presuming that Gelert had killed his son, slew him only later on to find the child sleeping beside a dead wolf, killed by the faithful Gelert. The reputed grave of Gelert can be seen in a field at the southern end of the village. From Beddgelert it is only a short walk to the famous Aberglaslyn Bridge and spectacular pass.

Beddgelert

Drawn by T. Compton & aquatinted by D. Havell

1816

CAERNARFONSHIRE 3

CRICCIETH

OS 123 : 498 376

In c.1230 Llywelyn ab Iorwerth began to build a castle at Criccieth. This consisted of the imposing double D-shaped gatehouse, the rectangular south-east tower and curtain wall surrounding the inner ward. Llywelyn ap Gruffydd then added the south-west tower, and the curtain wall enclosing the southern part of the outer ward. In 1283 Criccieth fell to the forces of Edward I, who then added another storey to the gatehouse and the northern engine tower. King Edward II also carried out further additions and improvements to the castle. In c.1404 Criccieth Castle was finally destroyed by Owain Glyndŵr, Prince of Wales, and was never rebuilt. Today Criccieth Castle is in the expert care of Cadw. Criccieth makes a good centre in order to visit Porthmadog, Portmeirion and the Llyn Peninsula.

Criccieth Castle

Watercolour by J.M.W. Turner

1836

CAERNARFONSHIRE 4

CAERNARFON CASTLE

OS 115 : 477 626

The massive castle and town walls of Caernarfon Castle (OS 115: 477 626) was built by Edward I in three main stages between 1283 and 1323. Edward II, the first Prince of Wales was born herein 1284. In 1403 Owain Glyndwr, the self styled Prince of Wales, unsuccessfully tried to capture the castle for the Welsh. More recently the castle was used for the investiture of Prince Edward (later King Edward VIII) as Prince of Wales, and again in 1969 for the investiture of Prince Charles.
Conwy Castle, (OS 115 : 477 626) just 24 miles further up the coast, is an equally grand castle was built on the site of a former Cistercian Abbey, which in 1245 was plundered by Henry III. In 1283 Edward I took the site over for the building of his castle and borough.

Caernarfon Castle from Anglesey

Drawn by T. Compton & engraved by D. Havell

1816

CAERNARFONSHIRE 5

BETWS Y COED, SWALLOW FALLS

OS 115 : 765 577

Betws y Coed can boast that it is in all probability the home of most visited waterfall in the whole of Wales. This is Rhaeadr Wennol or Swallow Falls, which in fact is a corruption of the Welsh Rhaeadr Ewynol, which means the 'Foaming Fall'. Most views of the falls only depict the first fall as the water cascades over a mass of rocks. This however, collects in a large pool before hurtling down a second magnificent fall. Close to Betws y Coed are two other fine waterfalls and well worth visiting the first is Conwy Falls (OS 116 : 809 535) and the second is Machno Falls or Pandy Fall (OS 116 : 808 533).

Swallow Falls or Rhaeadr Y Wennol

Drawn by F. Nicholson & aquatinted by T. Fielding

1820

CAERNARFONSHIRE 6

LLANBERIS

OS 115 : 602 586

Llanberis (OS 115 : 575 601) is the starting point for both the Snowdon Mountain Railway and one of the easiest walking routes to the top of Snowdon. Close to Llanberris can be seen Dolbadarn Castle (OS 115 : 586 598) picturesquely sited between beautiful lakes Padarn and Peris. This castle is particularly important as it is one of the best preserved of all the genuinely Welsh castles. It was built by Llywelyn ab Iorwerth c. 1200 in order to govern the ancient route from Caernarfon to the upper Conwy valley. The distinctive round stone keep has provided the ideal focal point for many great artists. Not far from the castle, and at the foot of the Snowdon Mountain Railway, is the splendid 80ft angular Ceunant Mawr Waterfall, (OS 115 : 578 593) which, when it is in spate, makes an amazing sight.

Llanberis Lake

Drawn by T. Compton & aquatinted by D. Havell

c. 1816

CAERNARFONSHIRE 7

DOLWYDDELAN CASTLE

OS 115 : 722 523

Ones first impression of this Welsh castle at Dolwyddelan Castle comes largely as a result of the nineteenth century restoration of the keep. The original keep was built by Llywelyn ab Iorwerth (The Great) c.1200 and this consisted of a basement and first floor apartment, reached by an external flight of steps, with a drawbridge and a small building protecting the entrance to the keep. The keep was later raised by another storey in the thirteenth century, probably by Edward I. The existing stone curtain wall may well have replaced an earlier timber palisade or fence in the early thirteenth century. In 1283 Edward I captured the castle from the Welsh and built a second tower, on the west side of the courtyard.

Dolwyddelan Castle

Coloured aquatint after T. H. Fielding & published by Thomas McLean

c.1823

CAERNARFONSHIRE 8

LLYN GWYNANT

OS 115 : 645 520

Thomas Compton writes. 'A short distance brought us to Llyn Gwynant, which is encompassed with mountains, but here they rise much more abruptly on the east, than on the same side of the other lake. On these, the rocks lie in immense detached masses, giving an air of extreme wildness to the scene, which is however softened by the verdure and the trees spread over the other parts. The view of the lake was taken from the road, about half a mile from the lower end, looking down.' There are equally good views of the Snowdonia range of mountains from Llyn Nant Lle (OS 115 : 515 530) and Llyn Dinas (OS 115 : 615 495).

Llyn Gwynant

Drawn by T. Compton & aquatinted by D. Havell

1816

CAERNARFONSHIRE 9

NANT FRANCON

OS 115 : 628 655

Thomas Compton writes as follows:- ‘Leaving the [Penrhyn] slate quarries, we proceeded on the high road up Nant Francon. This is undoubtedly one of the finest passes in Wales. The accompanying view is a faithful representation of the lower part of the hollow, and together with the view of the Cataract of Benglog, [Ogwen Falls, not shown] at the upper end, will give a correct idea of the scenery in this rude glen. The view was taken a short distance from the gate leading to Lady Penrhyn's secluded seat, Ogwen Bank. The beautiful grounds of this delightful retreat, form the foreground of the view; and beyond these, Glyder Vawr, Glyder Vach, and mountains branching from them, rear their lofty and rugged heads.’

Nant Francon

Drawn by T. Compton & aquatinted by D. Havell

1816

CAERNARFONSHIRE 10

YR WYDDFA FAWR OR SNOWDON

OS 115 : 609 544

For many the highlight of any visit to Caernarfonshire must be to have walked to the top of Snowdon, the highest mountain in England and Wales. The Snowdon range consists of a cluster of five peaks, linked by sharp ridges, and presenting fine escarpments in all directions, many of which over look remote mountain lakes. The highest of these peaks is Yr Wyddfa Fawr at 3,560 feet. The print shown above gives a splendid picture of the superb view from the top of Yr Wyddfa or Snowdon 'The King' of the Welsh mountains. Of course, today many people take the easy way out and catch the narrow-gauge rack and pinion train from Llanberis. This train journey on a fine day is a memorable experience and well worth the fare.

South view from the summit of Snowdon

Drawn by T. Compton & aquatinted by D. Havell

1816

THE ANCIENT COUNTY OF DENBIGHSHIRE

Castell Dinas Bran

Drawn by M. Griffith & engraved by W. Watts

c. 1780

By kind permission of Llyfrgell Genedlaethol Cymru / The National Library of Wales.

THE ANCIENT COUNTY OF DENBIGHSHIRE

1. Chirk Castle

2. Erddig

3. Dinas Bran

4. Denbigh Castle, Lord Leicester's Church & Friary

5. Llangollen & Plas Newydd

6. Llanrwst Bridge & Church

7. Pontcysyllte & Chirk Aqueducts

8. Valle Crucis Abbey

9. Wrexham Church

10. Ruthin Parish Church & Castle

DENBIGHSHIRE 1

CHIRK CASTLE

OS 126 : 271 381

Chirk Castle is a genuine medieval castle whose exterior has not changed much since it was built, except that the arrow slits have been enlarged into mullioned windows. During the War of the Roses and in the Civil War it was badly damaged but was repaired again after both occasions. Roger Mortimer began building the castle in 1295 and it was eventually completed in 1310 when it became the home of many powerful landowners, one of whom was Robert Dudley, Earl of Leicester. In 1595 the estate was bought by the prosperous goldsmith Sir Thomas Myddelton of Denbigh and it has remained the Myddleton Family home ever since. It is now in the care of the National Trust.

Chirk Castle

Drawn by H. Gastineau & engraved by J.C. Varrell

1816

DENBIGHSHIRE 2

ERDDIG HOUSE & GARDENS

OS 117 : 327 484

Joshua Edisbury built the original house at Erddig (the present central bays) between 1684-87. In c. 1716 John Meller, a London lawyer, acquired Erddig and added the two wings and collected most of the fine furniture that is still in the house today. Simon Yorke, the nephew of Meller, also assisted in this restoration and he inherited Erddig in 1733. It then remained in direct line with the Yorke family until 1973, when it was given to the National Trust, who began a mammoth and very successful restoration of the house and outbuildings more or less as they were when they inherited it from the Yorke family. The result is that one is given a clear picture of life in a country house in the early 20th century.

Erddig

Drawn by Evans & Engraved by Medland

1792

DENBIGHSHIRE 3

CASTELL DINAS BRAN

OS 117 : 224 431

Castell Dinas Bran was constructed in about 1260 by the local Welsh ruler, Prince Gruffudd ap Madoc on the site of a prehistoric hillfort. However, it had a very short life, for in May 1277, during Edward I's initial Welsh campaign, it was deliberately abandoned and fired by its Welsh garrison in order to prevent it being used by the English.
In Simpson's account of the Town and Vale of Llangollen, (1837), he writes *'The castle, is one of the primitive Welsh Castles and stands immediately above and on the north side of Llangollen, on a conical mountain, about seven hundred feet above the level of the Dee, and about one thousand feet above that of the sea; it is built on the summit of the hill, which probably was levelled to procure materials, as the building occupies the whole flat.'*

Castell Dinas Bran

Drawn by J. Laporte & aquatinted by Compte

1800

By kind permission of Llyfrgell Genedlaethol Cymru / The National Library of Wales.

DENBIGHSHIRE 4

DENBIGH CASTLE

OS 116 : 054 657

Denbigh Castle was once the residence of the Welsh Princes, but in 1282 it was superseded by the present castle, built for Henry de Lacey, Earl of Lincoln, having been given the site by Edward I. This castle consisted of a strong enclosure wall with seven towers, a massive gatehouse and town walls. Henry de Lacey also founded a fortified town within the town walls, which were over 1200 yards long and had four towers and two gateways. The Burgess Gate still stands, as does much of the wall. The St Hilary Tower is all that remains of the former parish church for those living within the walls. Just outside the walls can be seen the remains of Lord Leicester's Church (1578) which was never completed and on the outskirts of the town can be seen the remains of Denbigh Friary, a former Carmelite or White Friars friary founded in the late 13th century.

Denbigh Castle, Friary & Leicester's Church

Hand coloured copper engraving by Sparrow

1786

DENBIGHSHIRE 5

LLANGOLLEN

OS 117 : 215 422

Those who visit the town of Llangollen will have to cross the fine stone, four arched, bridge over the River Dee considered to be one of *'The Seven Wonders of Wales'*. The bridge was built in 1345 by John Trevor I, the Bishop of St Asaph, who lived at Trevor Hall on the outskirts of Llangollen. The bridge was rebuilt in the seventeenth century and widened in 1873 and in 1969. When the railway came to Llangollen the actual road over the bridge had to be raised in order to provide a further square arch over the new railway, which rather spoilt the perfect symmetry of the original bridge. The parish church is dedicated to St Collen and has two superb 15th century hammer beam roofs. Plas Newydd, the home of 'The Ladies of Llangollen' is also well worth a visit.

Llangollen Bridge & Castell Dinas Bran

Artist unknown & engraved by W. Batenham

19th century

DENBIGHSHIRE 6

LLANRWST

OS 116 : 800 615

Llanrwst is a small town deriving its name from St Grwst a 6th century missionary to whom the parish church is dedicated. The present church dates back to 1470 and has a fine rood screen and loft, which came from Maenan Abbey after the Dissolution. Adjoining the church is the grand 'Gwydir Chapel' built in 1633 by Sir Richard Wynne and said to have been designed by Inigo Jones. This chapel has an elaborate roof, panelling, screens and a number of fine tombs, including a stone coffin reputedly that of Llewelyn the Great. At Llanrwst there is a distinctive steep three-arched bridge over the River Conwy. This bridge was built in 1636 and, like the Gwydir Chapel; it is also thought to have been designed by Inigo Jones. The bridge was modified in 1703, but many feel that in doing so it lost much of its original character.

Llanrwst

Drawn & etched by J.G. Wood

1813

DENBIGHSHIRE 7

PONTCYSYLLTE AQUEDUCT

OS 117 : 270 421

The Pontcysyllte Aqueduct is a fantastic piece of waterway engineering as the Llangollen Canal is taken 1007 feet across the Dee valley. This is done at the amazing height of 126 feet above the River Dee and is supported by eighteen elegant arches carrying the huge iron water trough. Work began in 1795 and took ten years to complete. Although the aqueduct is generally attributed to Thomas Telford it was William Jessop who was the chief engineer of the project and constantly advised Telford. The aqueduct was eventually completed in 1805 with great ceremony and at a cost of £27,018. The Llangollen Canal continues from the Pontcysyllte Aqueduct for about three miles when it reaches the Chirk Aqueduct, which carries the canal 70 feet over the River Ceiriog, and was built by Telford in 1801 at a cost of £21,000.

Pontcysyllte Aqueduct

Drawn by Captain Batty & engraved by E. Finden

1823

DENBIGHSHIRE 8

VALLE CRUCIS ABBEY

OS 117 : 207 441

Valle Crucis Abbey, now in the care of Cadw, is the best preserved of the medieval monasteries in North Wales and takes its name *'The Vale of the Cross'* from the 7th century Pillar of Eliseg, which can be seen in a field just the north of the Abbey. This pillar originally stood 20 feet high and was surmounted with a cross. The Abbey was founded by Madoc ap Gruffydd in 1201, for the Cistercian 'White Monks' who set up a community here following the strict rules of their order. The shell of the cross-shaped abbey church is nearly complete, with a splendid west front, which has a triple lancet window, with a rose window above it and the west door below. The east front is also almost complete and has a fine set of five lancet windows. At the far end of the abbey grounds the original monks' fishpond is still well preserved. After a fire in the 15th century many of the domestic buildings were rebuilt.

Valle Crucis Abbey

Drawn Miss M. Smirke & aquatinted by J. Harriden

c. 1808

By kind permission of Llyfrgell Genedlaethol Cymru / The National Library of Wales.

DENBIGHSHIRE 9

WREXHAM

OS 117 : 335 505

The church of St Giles, Wrexham, considered as one of *the seven wonders of Wales,* is set in the centre of the busy county town The church is particularly noted for its superb steeple or tower. This 147ft tower was begun in 1506 and has four graceful hexagonal turrets and a number of medieval carvings of its patron saint St Giles. The pillars, arches and corbels in the nave were built in the 14th century, however in the 15th century the church was heightened and given present clear storey, carved roof, and a large east window. This east window was later altered and made into an entrance arch into the chancel. Wrexham church is well known to Americans, as it is the burial place of Elihu Yale (1648-1720) the founder of Yale University.

Wrexham Church

Drawn & engraved on wood by H. Hughes

1823

DENBIGHSHIRE 10

RUTHIN

OS 116 : 125 585

In the town of Ruthin there is a fine 14th century Parish Church dedicated to St Peter, with elaborate wrought iron churchyard gates. In 1310 Lord Grey of Ruthin created a collegiate church here, and the incumbent is still known as 'The Warden'. The choir was destroyed in 1663 and the spire was added in 1859. *(Note that the 1796 engraving below shows the church without the spire.)* The two roofs are particularly splendid, especially the one in the north aisle, which has over 400 carved panels and was given by King Henry VII as a thank offering to the people of Wales. Also in the town can be seen the remains of former Norman castle, which are now in the grounds of the modern Ruthin Castle Hotel.

Ruthin

Drawn by E. Pugh & engraved by W. Poole

1796

THE ANCIENT COUNTY OF FLINTSHIRE

Flint Castle

Drawn by J. Wrightson & engraved by W. Radclyffe

1836

THE ANCIENT COUNTY OF FLINTSHIRE

1. Basingwerk Abbey

2. Caergwrle & Hope Castles

3. Downing, Mr Pennant's Mill

4. Dyserth Waterfall

5. Flint Castle

6. Hawarden Castle

7. Holywell, St Winefride's Well

8. Overton Church

9. Rhuddlan Castle & Friary

10. St Asaph Cathedral

FLINTSHIRE 1

BASINGWERK ABBEY

OS 116 : 195 775

Near the coast at Greenfield can be seen the ruins of the former Basingwerk Abbey. Ranulph, Earl of Chester, founded Basingwerk Abbey in 1131 as a house of the Savignac Order, but in 1147 it became a Cistercian house. At the reformation the buildings were largely demolished and sold. The timber roof the choir went to St Mary's on the Hill in Chester, the timber of the refectory possibly to Cilcain, and the stained glass possibly to Dyserth. Today the best of the remains can be seen in the west wall, one of the crossing piers and in the monk's domestic buildings. In the refectory one can still see the remains of the former reader's pulpit. The ruins are now in the care of CADW and it has free entry.

Basingwerk Abbey

Drawn by M. Griffith & engraved by J. Caldwell

1790

FLINTSHIRE 2

CAERGWRLE & EWLOE CASTLES

OS 117 : 307 572

Caergwrle or Hope Castle, as it is often known, is a border Welsh castle situated on a former bronze-age hillfort, overlooking the villages of Caergwrle and Hope. Dafydd ap Gruffyudd, the brother of Llywelyn the Last, built the castle here between 1277 and 1282. Caergwrle Castle has taken the advantage of the strong natural defences of the site, which, with the formidable ditch on the north, completed its defences. Building works were still in progress when in 1282 Daffydd launched his final and fateful attack on Edward I's castle at Hawarden. The result of this was that Edward I presented Caergwrle Castle to Queen Eleanor. However, in 1283 it was accidentally burnt down, and soon afterwards abandoned. Another Welsh castle was built at Ewloe (OS 117 : 288 675), situated in a charming quiet woodland area just off a busy main road and overlooks the industrial district of Queensferry.

Caergwrle Castle

Drawn by & engraved by S. & N. Buck

1742

FLINTSHIRE 3

DOWNING, MR PENNANT'S MILL

OS 116 : 115 787

Thomas Pennant, the great topographical writer of 'Tours in Wales' which was first published in 1773, begins his introduction to Flintshire with the words *'I naturally begin my journey from the place of my nativity, Downing, in the township of Eden-Owain, in the parish of Whiteford, in the county of Flint.'* Thomas Pennant, and his father before him, lived at Downing Hall, which in 1812 the Revd. J. Evans describes as *'a good mansion in the form of a Roman H, with wings gabled, erected in the year 1627. It is placed in a low sequestered situation.'* (Sadly it is now demolished) The print below, taken from 'The Beauties of North Wales' depicts Mr Pennant's Mill, which in actual fact was a folly in the form of a ruined abbey or chapel built onto a former mill. Thomas Pennant died in 1798 and is buried in 'near the altar' in Whitford Church.

Mr Pennant's Mill at Downing

Drawn by T. Grose & engraved by Hay

1811

FLINTSHIRE 4

DYSERTH WATERFALL

OS 116 : 057 798

Right in the centre of the village at Dyserth there is a picturesque waterfall. Dyserth is an area, which is full of healthy springs in the limestone uplands above the village. It is these springs, rather than the small river that produce the fairly constant flow of water in the fall. At one time there was a working mill built close to the fall and one can still see the evidence of this former mill. Near the fall is the interesting church of St. Bridget and St. Cwyfan, which has a superb medieval stained glass east window, and may have come from Basingwerk Abbey at the Dissolution. The top part (c.1450) depicts the twelve apostles and the main section is of ‘a Jesse Tree’ (c.1530) depicting the lineage of Christ from Jesse, the father of King David.

Dyserth Waterfall

Vignette Newman & Co

c. 1870

FLINTSHIRE 5

FLINT CASTLE

OS 117 : 248 735

Flint Castle stands imposingly on the banks of the Dee shoreline and was the first in the chain of castles built by Edward I. These castles were built in order to defeat Prince Llywelyn and to halt his rugged determination for Welsh independence. Work on Flint Castle began in 1277 and was virtually finished by 1284. It consisted of a four-square ward with four round towers, one of which was much larger than the others, and had its own moat and drawbridge dominating the entrance to the castle. In 1399 Flint Castle was the final refuge of Richard II before he conceded the crown to Henry IV. It changed hands several times during the Civil War and finally fell to Parliament in 1646 and then into disuse. Close to Flint Castle can be seen the remains of the beautifully situated Welsh castle at Ewloe (OS 117 : 288 675), which was built by Llwelyn ap Gruffudd in c.1257.

Flint Castle

Drawn by H. Gastineau & engraved by S. Lacey

1831

FLINTSHIRE 6

HAWARDEN CASTLE

OS 117 : 316 655

In 1282 the Welsh Prince Dafydd, the brother of Llywelyn, attacked Hawarden Castle because it was a strategically placed Borderland castle on the main road from Chester to North Wales, and, until 1804, literally passed beneath its ramparts. Hawarden Castle was built on an ancient hill fort, which was re-used for the Norman mote and bailey built by Hugh, the Earl of Chester. In 1265 Prince Llywelyn destroyed this castle and in 1282 a new English castle began to be built, which prompted the attack by Dafydd. Today the ruins of the castle, with its splendidly preserved keep, are in private ownership and can only be visited when the gardens of the crenellated mansion are open. This mansion was once the home of Prime Minister William Gladstone (1809-1898) and now of his descendants.

Hawarden Castle

Drawn & etched by J.G. Wood

1813

FLINTSHIRE 7

HOLYWELL ST WINEFRIDE'S WELL

OS 116 : 184 764

Wales has many Holy Wells, which in the past were much visited as places of healing and prayer. This was particularly true of **St Winefride's Well,** from which the town of **Holywell** takes its name, and is included as one of *'The Seven Wonders of Wales'*. The origins of the well, according to legend, go back to the 7th century when a rejected suitor beheaded the Welsh Princess Gwefrewi (Winefride). The head, legend says, bounced down the hill to a spring. Her uncle St Beuno then picked it up and replaced the head on her neck and so restored Winefride's life for another 15 years! A shrine was then built on the spot and throughout the Middle Ages pilgrims flocked here for healing. In about 1500 Margaret Beaufort, the mother of Henry VII, rebuilt the shrine to its present splendour. Even after the Reformation the shrine still was used as a place of pilgrimage and healing and still remains so today.

St Winefride's Well

Drawn by H. Gastineau Engraved by W. Wallis

1831

FLINTSHIRE 8

OVERTON CHURCH

OS 117 : 373 418

The three great Parish churches of Overton, Wrexham and Gresford are all included in the rhyme *'The Seven Wonders of Wales'*, a title that all three churches richly deserve. Wrexham is remembered for its superb steeple or tower and Gresford is remembered for its bells. However, St Mary's, Overton is remembered for its ancient yew trees, some of which are thought to date back 1500-2000 years. The church tower is 14th century and houses a set of six bells and a fine clock. The Norman circle cross, built into the west pillar of the church is thought to be the oldest stonework in the church. Also look out for the 15th century oak chest and a 6th century Abyssinian brass processional cross.

Overton Church

Drawn by H. Gastineau & engraved by W. Radclyffe

1830

FLINTSHIRE 9

RHUDDLAN CASTLE

OS 116 : 025 778

The castle at Rhuddlan was one of the distinctive concentric castles built by Edward I on the north Welsh coast, and was closely followed by the castles at Conwy, Harlech and Beaumaris. These castles consist of three concentric rings of fortification rather than the traditional keep. The innermost of this fortification consists of a diamond-plan strong hold, with a twin-towered gatehouse at two corners and a single round tower at the others. Beyond this is there is an outer circuit of lower turreted walls, and beyond this a deep moat, which was linked with the River Clwyd. The castle is now in the care of Cadw, who have produced an excellent guidebook to the castle. Close to Rhuddlan castle is a footpath to Twthill motte and bailey, which was once the site of the Norman precursor to the new castle built by Edward.

Rhuddlan Castle

Drawn by Captain Batty & engraved by E. Finden

1823

FLINTSHIRE 10

ST ASAPH CATHEDRAL

OS 116 : 037 743

St Asaph Cathedral was founded by St Kentigern and, has been a site of Christian worship since AD 560. Asaph, who gave his name to the city and to the diocese, succeeded Bishop Kentigern in 570. The present building is a mixture of architecture dating from the 13th-14th centuries, giving a blend of simplicity, quiet dignity and beauty. The roof is much later than the rest of the building and was restored and decorated in 1968. The Presbytery contains the Bishop's Throne and beneath the throne is the burial place of Bishop William Morgan, who translated the bible into Welsh in 1588 and was Bishop of St Asaph from 1601-1604. The finely carved stalls date from 1482. Outside the Cathedral one can clearly see how two different types of stone have been used for building the cathedral, which unfortunately are reacting with each other and are gradually wearing each other away!

St. Asaph Cathedral

Vignette steel engraving, published by T. Catherall, Chester

c. 1860

THE ANCIENT COUNTY OF MERIONETHSHIRE

Cwm Maintwrog

Drawn by T. Compton & engraver unknown

1815

THE ANCIENT COUNTY OF MERIONETHSHIRE

1. Bala Lake

2. Castell Prysor & Castell y Bere

3. Barmouth

4. Cader Idris

5. Dolgellau & Cymer Abbey

6. Vale of Ffestiniog, Rhaeadr Cwm & Cynfal

7. Rug & Llangar Churches

8. Rhaeadr Ddu

9. Harlech Castle

10. Tal-y-Llyn, Bird Rock & Tywyn

MERIONETHSHIRE 1

BALA LAKE

OS 125 : 915 340

Thomas Compton in 1815 describes Bala Lake as follows :- *Its length in a direction nearly south west, is about four miles; its breadth about three quarters of a mile. The tour of it, eleven or twelve miles, affords the greatest variety of scenery. To the south, the lower parts consist of meadows and cornfields. To the north and west, the wood and rock are more mixt with the cultivated parts. To the east there are the meadows at the upper part of the beautiful vale of the Dee, and the town of Bala. In the distance is the triple headed Cader Idris.* Although, today there are more houses and tourist amenities around Bala Lake than there were in the time of Thomas Compton, one can still recapture the picturesque scene as painted by him in 1815.

Bala Lake

Drawn by T. Compton & aquatinted by J. Baily

1815

MERIONETHSHIRE 2

CASTELL PRYSOR & CASTELL Y BERE

OS 124 : 758 369

Castell Prysor is a remote Motte and Bailey site, which once was a Welsh castle. The motte is formed of a natural rock out-crop and was heightened with masonry. Within the bailey there are the foundations of various buildings. The date and origins of the former castle are uncertain but are probably late 12th century and possibly the work of Gruffudd ap Cynan c.1188. The only documentary evidence of the castle is a letter sent from there in 1284 by Edward I (Private land). Another Welsh castle in Merionethshire is Castell y Bere (OS 124 : 667 085) is beautifully situated at the foot of the Cader Idris mountain range and looks out towards Cardigan Bay. The castle was begun c.1221 by Llywelyn ab Iorwerth (the Great). In 1283 Edward I captured the castle and refurbished it, and it was finally burnt down in 1294.

Castell Prysor

Copper engraving probably after Moses Griffith

c.1784

By kind permission of Llyfrgell Genedlaethol Cymru / The National Library of Wales.

MERIONETHSHIRE 3

BARMOUTH

OS 124 : 615 156

The picture painted of Barmouth in 1816 by Thomas Compton and engraved by Daniel Havell, as shown above, is very different from the Barmouth of today. In 1816 Barmouth was a small seaside town and attempts were made to make it a place for the export of Welsh products, but ships of any size were prevented from entering the harbour because of the bar at the mouth of the river. Today Barmouth is a busy and popular seaside resort, largely due to the extensive sandy beach. From Barmouth it is worthwhile to walk up to the Panorama Walk, where, at about 400ft, there are superb views over the Mawddach estuary and the surrounding area between Dolgellau and the coast.

Abermaw or Barmouth

Drawn by T. Compton & aquatinted by D. Havell

1816

MERIONETHSHIRE 4

CADER IDRIS

OS 124 : 709 131

When the artist Thomas Compton had his first views of Cader Idris he wrote '*From here, the whole [of Cader Idris] is seen from the base to the summit, rising to the height of about 2800ft above the valley, the summit being 2914ft above the level of the sea. As we approached, the appearance of the mountain gradually changed, the nearer parts apparently rising and those farther off lowering in proportion. Now and then a light cloud would float past, for a time cutting off the summit, and then resting on the side of the mountain.*' The view shown below was taken about three quarters of a mile from the base of Cader Idris, and two and a half miles from the summit, which appears considerably lower than it really is because of the distance involved.

Pen y Cader or Cader Idris

Drawn by T. Compton & aquatinted by D. Havell

1816

MERIONETHSHIRE 5

DOLGELLAU

OS 124 : 729 177

The busy tourist town of Dolgellau, nestling at the foot of Cader Idris, makes the ideal centre for those visiting Southern Snowdonia. One enters the pleasant small town, from the north, via a fine seven-arched bridge c.1638. Dolgellau is particularly well known for two excellent walks. The first is Torrent Walk, which follows the River Clywedog as it tumbles down the hill to join Afon Wnion and Dolgellau in a series of small waterfalls. The second is Precipice Walk, which at about 1000ft above the River Mawddach gives the most superb views of Cader Idris and the Barmouth estuary. On the outskirts of Dolgellau are the remains of Cymer Abbey (OS 124 : 723 195) a 14th century Cistercian house founded in c.1199 and dissolved in 1536.

Dolgellau

Drawn by J.P. Neale & aquatinted by Matthews

1813

MERIONETHSHIRE 4

FFESTINIOG

OS 124 : 704 419

The village of Ffestiniog, situated between the Vale of Ffestiniog and the Vale of Cynfal, makes a good base for visiting several places of interest in the locality. These should include the viewpoint looking down on Rhaeadr Cwm, as Afon Cynfal tumbles down towards the Vale of Ffestiniog in a series of dramatic waterfalls. Two miles further down the river and near the village of Ffestiniog are two more waterfalls known as Rhaeadr Cynfal. Between the falls there is a remarkable large rock standing high in the middle of the river known as Pulpit Huw Llwyd, a local mystic who is supposed to have preached from the top of the rock.

The Vale of Ffestiniog

Drawn by J.P. Neale & engraved by J. Grieg

1812

MERIONETHSHIRE 7

RUG & LLANGAR CHURCHES

OS 125 : 064 439 & 125 : 063 426

The private chapel at Rug was built in 1637 and the remarkable colourful interior remains much the same today as it did in 1637. It is a rare example of the 'high church' liturgical experiments of Charles I. The chief glory of Rug Chapel is its highly decorated and carved roof.

The isolated, recently restored, church of All Saints, Llangar has a fine medieval wooden roof and several crude wall paintings. The furnishings of the church are mostly Georgian and include a fine three-decker pulpit, simple box pews for the gentry and benches for the villagers. In the gallery, used for a choir and musicians, there is an unusual four-sided music stand.

Llangar Church

Watercolour by John Ingleby

1794

By kind permission of Llyfrgell Genedlaethol Cymru / The National Library of Wales.

MERIONETHSHIRE 8

RHAEADR DDU

OS 124 : 720 245

On the main road from Dollgellau to Ffestiniog one should stop to visit the famous waterfall at Ganllwyd, known as Rhaeadr Ddu or the Black Waterfall, now in the care of the National Trust. Thomas Compton describes the scene as follows:-'*After a delightful walk of about quarter of a mile on the rocky bank of this impetuous river, Rhaiadyr Du burst suddenly upon us. The river rises in the mountains not far off, and after running over the rocks for some distance, arrives at the upper precipice, whence it is projected, in two full streams, from a height of forty feet, into a bed of black and rugged rock. Struggling through this, it at length bursts out in a collected stream, into a basin nearly surrounded by dark and perpendicular rocks. In front of, and just above the basin, the view is taken.*'

Rhaeadr Ddu

Drawn by T. Compton & engraver unknown

1815

MERIONETHSHIRE 9

HARLECH CASTLE

OS 124 : 577 313

The small, busy town of Harlech has become particularly popular because of the fine castle in the center of the town. The castle is built some 200ft above the superb sandy Harlech beach and the extensive marshes of Morfa Harlech. It also overlooks the Welsh Castle at Criccieth on the other side of the estuary. Harlech Castle is a remarkably complete and a well preserved example of Edward I system of concentric fortification. It was built between 1283 and 1289 and received its charter as an English borough in 1285. In 1404 it was captured by Owen Glendower, Prince of Wales, and for four years served as his capital, until it was retaken by the English 1408.

Harlech Castle

Drawn by M. Alstone & lithographed by W. Day

c. 1815

MERIONETHSHIRE 10

TAL-Y-LLYN

OS 124 : 715 100

The countryside around Tal-y-Llyn, lying beneath the southern slopes of Cader Idris, is an area that is full of interest. To the north-east is the hamlet of Minffordd, which is the start of the most popular route to Cader Idris. To the north-west are the remains of Castel-y-Bere the site of a former Welsh castle built c.1221 by Llywelyn ab Iorwerth and later captured by Edward I, who refurbished it. It was finally burnt down in 1294. Castel-y-Bere looks down the Dysynni valley to the distinctive 'Bird Rock' and to the charming seaside town of Tywyn. At Tywyn the Tal-y-Llyn narrow gauge railway has it terminus and the line goes as far as Nant Gwernol, via the triple waterfall at Dolgoch.

Tal-y-Llyn

Drawn by H. Gastineau & engraved by H. Adlard

1830

THE ANCIENT COUNTY OF MONTGOMERYSHIRE

Ruins of Montgomery Castle from the Severn

Coloured lithograph, published by G. & W.B. Whittkaer

1823

THE ANCIENT COUNTY OF MONTGOMERYSHIRE

1. Llanidloes

2. Dovey Mill & Fall

3. Dolforwyn Castle

4. Machynlleth

5. Montgomery Castle

6. Montgomery Town

7. Newtown

8. Pistyll Rhaeadr

9. Powis Castle

10. Welshpool

MONTGOMERYSHIRE 1

LLANIDLOES

OS 136 : 954 848

The small town of Llanidloes is situated at the confluence of the River Severn (or Hafren) and the River Clywedog. The main feature of Llanidloes is the half-timbered free-standing Old Market Hall c.1600. The upper floor was originally as a court house and then in the 18th and 19th centuries became a meeting place for the Quakers, Methodists and the Baptists before they built their own chapels. Outside the Market Hall there is a stone from which John Wesley preached during his three visits to the town. The parish church, dedicated to the 7th century St. Idloes, was restored and enlarged in 1881 but still retains many original features. It is thought that the finely carved 13th century north arcade and the15th century hammer-beam roof both came from Cwmhir Abbey at the Dissolution. Llanidloes makes a good centre for visiting the Hafren Forest and Llyn Clywedog.

Llanidloes Church & Bridge

Ink & wash drawing by Thomas Sunderland

c.1800

By kind permission of the National Museum of Wales

MONTGOMERYSHIRE 2

DOVEY FURNACE & FALL

OS 135 : 686 952

Dovey Furnace and the waterfall are particularly well known simply because they are only a few yards away from the main road from Aberystwyth to Machynlleth. The waterfall was artificially raised in order to give a greater head of water to the water wheel below the fall. Originally (hence the name of the village) this was used in the 16th century for refining silver and the 17th century as a blast furnace for the manufacture of iron. J.G. Wood wrote in 1813 *'Dovey Furnace was erected in about the year 1755 by an English company, and continued to work for many year, using iron ore that came from Lancashire.'* However, as J.G. Wood states, it was deserted by 1813. Recently Cadw has carefully restored the whole site, together with a new working water wheel.

Dovey Furnace

Soft ground etching drawn & etched by J.G.Wood

1813

MONTGOMERYSHIRE 3

DOLFORWYN CASTLE

OS 136 : 152 951

Dolforwyn Castle is sited on a rocky platform at the top of a steep ridge overlooking the Severn Valley. It was a Welsh castle, of the Princes of Gwynedd, and fortified by Llywelyn ap Gruffudd in 1273 as a stronghold against both the English and the Princes of Powys. It played a particularly important part in the history of Llywelyn ap Gruffydd, the last native Prince of Wales, as it was the only castle to have been entirely built as a new foundation by Llywelyn himself. It was also strategically important, as it was close to Edward I's castle at Montgomery. Recently Cadw have carried out extensive excavation and repair work, which gives a much more comprehensive plan of the original castle.

Dolforwyn Dastle

Watercolour by Moses Griffiths

1796

By kind permission of Llyfrgell Genedlaethol Cymru / The National Library of Wales.

MONTGOMERYSHIRE 4

MACHYNLLETH

OS 135 : 746 008

The town of Machynlleth is situated in the green valley of the Dyfi and is a centre serving a wide district set in the heart of much beautiful Welsh scenery. In the centre of the town is the distinctive clock tower, which was erected in 1872. In Maengwyn Street one can visit the Owain Glyndŵr Centre, a 16th century building which was built on the site where Owain Glyndŵr, the self styled Prince of Wales, set up his independent parliament in 1404. On the opposite side of the road is Plas Machynlleth, which with its fine grounds, was presented to the town by Lord Londonderry. Until recently this was the site of The Celtic Centre but sadly this has now closed and is now in a state of neglect. However, one should still look out for the elegant monument in Welsh slate carved by Ieuan Rees that was erected in 2000 to commemorate thy 600th anniversary of the proclamation of Owain Glyndŵr as Prince of Wales.

Owain Glyndŵr's Parliament Building at Machynlleth

Drawn by E. Pugh & aquatinted by T. Cartwright

1814

MONTGOMERYSHIRE 5

MONTGOMERY CASTLE

OS 137 : 217 969

In 1233 the stone built castle, high up and looking down on the town at Montgomery succeeded the motte and bailey at Hen Domen. This new castle was built as a result of Henry III's campaign against Llywelyn ap Iorwerth. The entrance to the Castle is by the modern bridge over an outer ditch, leading into the middle ward, where there are remains of two round towers either side of the gatehouse. A second bridge leads into the inner ward, which also has two round towers. Inside this inner ward there is D-shaped tower, the castle well, the remains of the kitchens and brew-house and a round tower at its far end.

Montgomery Castle

Drawn & etched by Samuel & Nathaniel Buck

1742

MONTGOMERYSHIRE 6

MONTGOMERY TOWN

OS 137 : 224 965

Below Montgomery Castle lies the attractive Georgian styled town of Montgomery. The parish church is basically 13th century but the tower was restored in the 19th century. Inside the church there is a fine double screen, loft, stalls and misericords, which are thought to have come from the former Austin Canons Priory at Chirbury, two and a half miles north east (in England). Also in the church are some good examples of Renaissance tombs in memory of the Herbert and Mortimer families. Offa's Dyke was cut through Montgomery in about 784 and a section of this has been preserved in Lymore Park, east of the town.

Montgomery

Drawn by H. Gastineau & engraved by J.C. Varrall

1835

MONTGOMERYSHIRE 7

NEWTOWN

OS 136 : 110 914

When Dolforwyn Castle was destroyed in 1277 (by the Mortimers of Montgomery Castle), it is likely that a new market town was established in order to replace the one that used to be held outside the walls of the old castle. This explains why the new town became known as Newtown or in Welsh Y Drenewydd. Newtown was protected by a motte and bailey, remains of which can still be seen in The Park. In 1280 Edward I granted the borough a charter, which marked the start of a commercial growth, which peaked in the 19th century, when the town had become a centre for weaving and the home of the Welsh flannel industry. But by 1830 Newtown was beginning to face heavy competition from the large new factories in Lancashire and Yorkshire, which meant the inevitable closure of many of its small factories and considerable local hardship. Today Newtown is a thriving modern town with a population that exceeds that at the height of the woollen industry.

Newtown, Montgomeryshire, from the Bryn Bank

Drawn by G. Hillier & lithographed by E. Noyce

1846

By kind permission of Llyfrgell Genedlaethol Cymru / The National Library of Wales.

MONTGOMERYSHIRE 8

PISTYLL RHAEADR

OS 125 : 073 296

Pistyll Rhaeadr is included as one of the *'Seven Wonders of Wales'*, due to the fact that it is thought to be the highest waterfall in Wales. The remarkably small Afon Disgynfa make a magnificent drop of 240ft in two great leaps. The first of these is a near vertical torrent of water which is broken 80ft from the bottom by a small band or rock, fronted by a natural arch, through which the river then pours out in a deep mass of white foam for its final descent into the deep pool at its base. George Borrow in his Book 'Wild Wales' writes *'There are many remarkable cataracts in Britain, but this Rhaeadr, the grand cataract of North Wales, exceeds them all. I never saw water falling so gracefully, so much like thin beautiful threads as here.'*

Pistyll Rhaeadr

Drawn by T. Compton & aquatinted by J. Baily

1815

MONTGOMERYSHIRE 9

POWIS CASTLE

OS 126 : 216 062

The Princes of Powys first established Powis Castle in the 13th century when it was built from the craggy outcrop of red gritstone on which it now stands. The design followed the traditional Norman style, with a strong keep (the present castle), an inner bailey (the entrance courtyard) and a massive outer wall. The oldest parts of the castle (c.1200) are the twin drum towers at the entrance. Over the last 400 years this former medieval fortress, which was originally built for war, has been transformed into a grand dwelling place, and the home of the great Herbert and Clive dynasties, who still live in part of the castle, which is now in the care of the National Trust. On the five terraces below the castle are the superb gardens, which combine 18th century lead statues and huge clipped yew trees with various formal gardens, inspired by the baroque gardens of France and Italy.

Powis Castle

Drawn by Grose & engraved by White

1813

MONTGOMERYSHIRE 10

WELSHPOOL

OS 126 : 225 075

Welshpool or Y Trallwng owes it name to a charter granted to the town by the Prince of Powys in 1263 This charter was largely a confirmation of earlier privileges, notably the authority to hold a Monday market, which is still in force today. St Mary's Church was restored in 1871 but still shows evidence of work dating back to the 13th century particularly in the west tower and the choir. At Canal Wharf one can visit the Powysland Museum and Canal Centre, which gives an excellent history of Montgomeryshire from prehistoric times to today. Welshpool is about half way along the former Montgomeryshire Canal, which was built three stages between 1796 and 1821, but abandoned by 1944. Today parts of the canal have been reopened and short narrowboat cruises can be taken from Canal Wharf. Also, short steam train trips from the station can be made on the Welshpool & Llanfair Railway.

Welshpool, from the Park of Powis Castle

Drawn by H. Gastineau & engraved by J.C. Varrall

1831

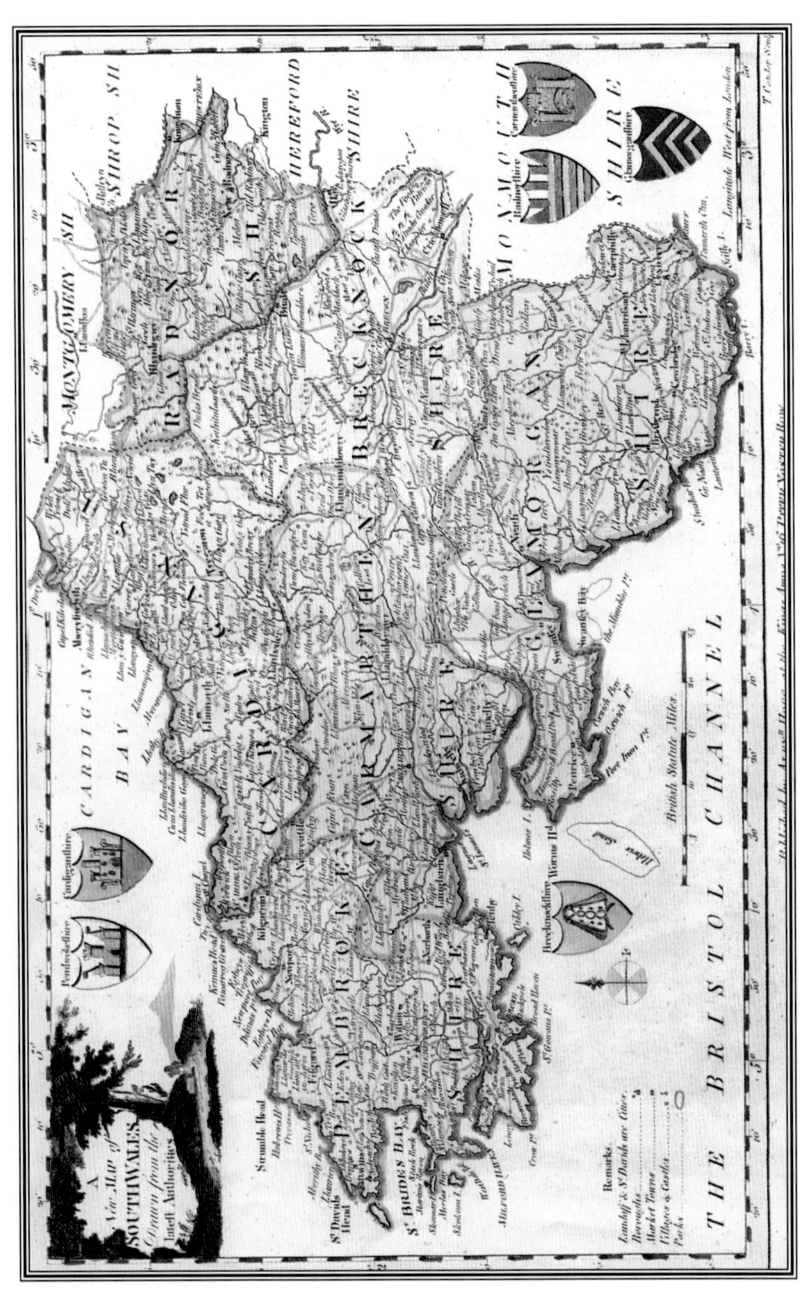

Map of South Wales 1794

THE SIX ANCIENT COUNTIES OF SOUTH WALES & MONTMOUTHSHIRE

1. BRECKOCKSHIRE

2. CARMARTHENSHIRE

3. CARDIGANSHIRE

4. GLAMORGANSHIRE

5. PEMBROKESHIRE

6. RADNORSHIRE

****

7. MONMOUTHSHIRE

THE ANCIENT COUNTY OF BRECKNOCKSHIRE

Brecon Cathedral

Drawn by D. Cox & engraved by W. Radclyffe

c.1836

THE ANCIENT COUNTY OF BRECKNOCKSHIRE

1. Brecon

2. Brecon Beacons

3. Bronllys Castle

4. Crickhowell

5. Hay

6. Henrhyd Fall

7. Llangorse Lake

8. Tretower Castle

9. Porth y Ogof

10. Ystradfellte Waterfalls

BRECKNOCKSHIRE 1

BRECON

OS 160 : 045 290

The town of Brecon has several places of interest and these include the Cathedral, which began its life as a Benedictine Priory and was founded by Bernard of Newmarch at the close of the 11th century. Brecon Castle was also founded by Bernard of Newmarch and was originally a simple motte and bailey structure. The walls of this first fortress were later partly built with the stones from the old Roman station of Caerbannau, (Y Gaer), which was the Welsh capital of Brycheiniog. As well as having a cathedral church and a castle Brecon also has a fine bridge spanning the Honddu just below the castle before it joins the Usk in the town. Near the junction of these two rivers can be seen the remains of a former Dominican Friary, founded in 1250. The Friary was revived, in the nineteenth century, as Christ's College, which now uses the Friary Choir as its college chapel.

Brecon Bridge

Drawn by G. Samuel & engraved by J. Storer

1791

BRECKNOCKSHIRE 2

BRECON BEACONS

OS 160 : 013 216

The highest and most distinctive of all the Beacons is Pen y Fan and the most popular route to it is from Storey Arms (A470). On the approach to the summit one arrives first at Corn Du (873m) and then on to Pen y Fan (886m). The views here, on a clear day, are absolutely superb, for one can have a panoramic view of the whole of the Brecon Beacons National Park. Another popular approach to Pen y Fan is from the village of Ffwdgrech, where one more or less follows Cwm Llwch. This is a much more attractive route, but is steeper towards the summit. Near Ffwdgrech there is a fine waterfall at Pont Ryrd Goch and, as one begins the steep ascent to Pen y Fan, one can look down on the mysterious glacial lake, Llyn Cwm Llwch.

The Brecon Beacons

Watercolour by General Roy & Mudge

1821

By kind permission of Llyfrgell Genedlaethol Cymru / The National Library of Wales.

BRECKNOCKSHIRE 3

BRONLLYS CASTLE

OS 161 : 150 347

Just outside the small village of Bronllys, beside the River Llynfi and close to the main road can be seen the ancient remains of Bronllys Castle. This castle was first established with a motte and bailey by Richard Fitz Pons in the late 11th century. In the 13th century the impressive tower was added by Walter de Clifford. This tower has recently been restored by CADW and there is now good access to the top, which clearly shows the signs of its former use as a residence. From the top of the tower there are some good views looking towards the Black Mountains.

Bronllys Castle

Wood engraving by H. Hughes

1823

BRECKNOCKSHIRE 4

CRICKHOWELL

OS 1161 : 218 182

The River Usk is particularly wide at Crickhowell and is crossed by a superb narrow arched bridge, which today can cause considerable traffic hold ups. It is well worth finding time to stop and view this beautiful bridge, which is known to have been in existence in 1538. The bridge was rebuilt in 1706 with local stone and is curious in that it has thirteen arches on one side and twelve on the other, but this was the result of further restoration work done in 1830. On the south side of the town, close to the A40, are the remains of Alisby's Castle, which was built in 1272 by Sir Grimbald Pauncefort. It passed into several different hands until it eventually came into the possession of Roger Mortimer. Its name derives from his ally Alisby, who was given the castle as a thank offering for Mortimer's release from the Tower of London.

Crickhowell

Drawn & etched by J.G. Wood

1811

BRECKNOCKSHIRE 5

HAY-ON-WYE

OS 161 : 228 422

As Hay-on-Wye is a border town it is not surprising to find it has a castle. Originally there was a castle near the parish church, where there are still traces of a motte. In about 1200 a Norman castle was built on the site of the present castle in the centre of the town. Today only part of the walls and a thirteenth century gateway survive of the original castle. This is mainly due to the fact that in the seventeenth century a large mansion was built within its walls. In Victorian days this mansion was used as a vicarage for the Vicar of Hay. More recently two fires have considerably damaged the building. Hay-on-Wye is now world famous as a town of second hand books and people come from far and wide to look at the vast number of bookshops that can be found in the town.

Hay-on-Wye

Drawn by D. Cox & engraved by W. Radclyffe

1837

BRECKNOCKSHIRE 6

HENRHYD FALLS

OS 160 : 854 120

The River Llech is a very minor river, but it produces the most splendid 90ft Henrhyd Waterfall, which drops in a single fall on its way to join the River Tawe. This fall is thought to be the highest single drop of any waterfall south of Devil's Bridge. It is interesting to see a thin layer of coal in the rock behind the fall, a reminder of the former coal mining industry in this area. The best view of the fall is from about halfway down the public footpath, through the trees and on a sunny autumn day. Today Henrhyd Fall and its surrounds are in the care of the National Trust who has made the approach to the fall so much more accessible.

Henrhyd Fall

Watercolour W.W. Young

1832

By kind permission of Llyfrgell Genedlaethol Cymru / The National Library of Wales.

BRECKNOCKSHIRE 7

LLANGORSE LAKE

OS 161 : 130 265

On the north west side of Llangorse Lake there is a man-made island or crannog, known as Bwlch. This island has been built from a large heap of stones and is thought to have been an Iron Age settlement. Giraldus Cambrensis is supposed to have visited Llangorse Lake on his tour of Wales and claimed that the birds here only sang to the true ruler of the principality. He also considered that the water of the lake had magical powers in that at times it appeared green and at other times it appeared to be tinged with blood red veins. In actual fact the water only looked red because the River Llynfi flows into the lake over red sandstone, which at times can leave a trail of discolouration!

The Church & Pool

Drawn by J.P. Neale & engraved by Hay

c.1815

BRECKNOCKSHIRE 8

TRETOWER CASTLE

OS 161 : 185 212

Tretower Castle began its life as a twelfth century motte founded by a Norman knight called Picard. The Welsh then captured this Norman stronghold in 1233, but it soon reverted back to the English when the uprising was crushed. It was probably at this time that the bailey was added, with a stone surrounding wall with three small towers, and a tall round central keep. In the 14th century a manor house was built close to the castle. In the 15th century both the Castle and the Manor House passed into the hands of Sir Roger Vaughan, who began to rebuild and created a new fortified manor house, which replaced the castle as their family home. Over the years many alterations have been made, but the original manor has survived and is now in the care of Cadw.

Tretower Castle

Drawn & etched by J.G.Wood

1811

BRECKNOCKSHIRE 9

PORTH Y OGOF

OS 160 : 927 122

Near the village of Ystradfellte, one can view the impressive entrance to a vast underground cave system known as Porth yr Ogof. Here the River Mellte goes underground for nearly three-quarters of a mile. The entrance to the cave is one of the largest in Wales and is a favourite venue for experienced cavers. The bed of the River Mellte is usually dry here, but after heavy rain it can quickly become a raging torrent. Only those who have a good knowledge of the cave should go any distance inside, for it can present all sorts of dangers. There is a passage to the right of the main entrance, which leads to a remarkable cavern of about 6000 square feet. The ceiling of this immense cavern is completely flat and has no means of support other than the sides of the cave. The river emerges again half a mile upstream at the Blue Pool.

Porth y Ogof

Sepia watercolour W.W. Young

c.1830

By kind permission of The National Museum of Wales.

BRECKNOCKSHIRE 10

YSTRADFELLTE WATERFALLS

OS 160 : 930 135

Between Ystradfellte and Pontneddfechan there are four rivers which all have superb waterfall walks. The first is the River Mellte on which there are three fine falls, known as Sgwd Clyn-gwyn, Sgwd Isaf Clyn-gwyn and Sgwd y Pannwr. The second is the River Hepste, which has two more splendid falls known as the Lower Cilhepste and Sgwd yr Eira (probably the best known of all the falls in this area). The third is the River Pyrddin, which has two falls called Sgwd Gwladys and Sgwd Einion Gam (a difficult fall to find as it involves crossing the river several times). Finally on the River Nedd there are three more exciting falls and are called the Horseshoe Falls, Lower Sgwd Ddwli, and Upper Sgwd Ddwli. All these splendid falls are well worth visiting.

Cilhepste Waterfall

Coloured etching by W.W. Young

1835

THE ANCIENT COUNTY OF CARMARTHENSHIRE

Carreg Cennan Castle

Drawn & engraved on wood by H. Hughes

1823

THE ANCIENT COUNTY OF CARMARTHENSHIRE

1. Aberglasney

2. The Black Mountain

3. Carmarthen

4. Dinefwr Park & Castle

5. Kidwelly Church & Castle

6. Laugharne & Llansteffan Castles

7. Llandovery & Llandeilo

8. Llandybie Glynhir Waterfall

9. Newcastle Emlyn Castle

10. Talley Abbey

CARMARTHENSHIRE 1

ABERGLASNEY

OS 159 : 580 221

The nine gardens of Aberglasney have a long and interesting history and were first mentioned by a 15th century bard and reached in their heyday c.1890. But, in spite its long and varied history, both the house and the garden fell into a complete state of neglect. However, in the 1990s a miracle of transformation was seen to begin as the historic gardens, with their streams and ponds, began to be restored to their former glory. Restoration has also begun to be done on the house and outbuildings. The gardens and woodlands are now open to the public and go to make a delightful day out. There is also an excellent restaurant on site, which sells many tasty homemade meals to the growing number of visitors to Aberglasney.

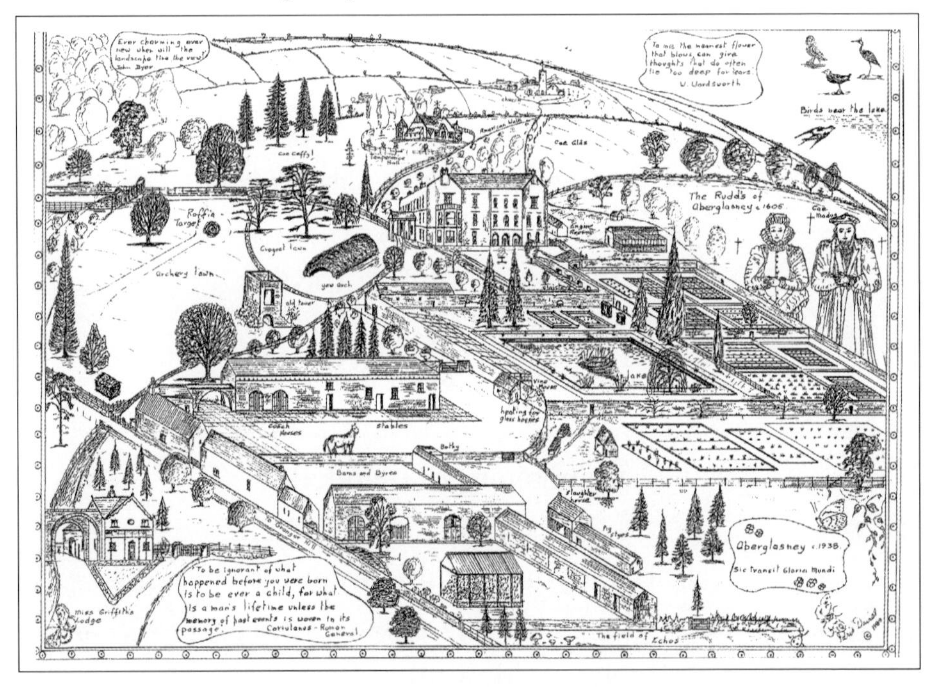

An artistic bird's-eye impression of Aberglasney c.1938
Similar to the design by Dyer family c.1710-1803

Drawn by Idris Davies 1989

Reproduced by kind permission of the artist, Idris Davies

CARMARTHENSHIRE 2
THE BLACK MOUNTAIN

OS 160 : 805 220

The easiest way to the Black Mountain is from Llanddeusant where there is a small medieval church that has been built on the site of an earlier monastery, which tradition says was founded by St. Paulinus, the tutor of St. David. The evidence for the church's ancient origin is largely due to the discovery here of a 7th century slab cross. Llanddeusant village is popular for both climbers and walkers to Bannau Sir Gaer (749m) and Fan Brycheiniog (802m), the highest point on the Black Mountain. From the village there is an easy and rewarding walk along a stony track to the beautiful Llyn y Fan Fach, which nestles comfortably below the dramatic escarpment of Bannau Sir Gaer, and is the gateway to this almost unknown part of the Black Mountain. The three major rivers, the Usk, Tawe and Twrch, all have their source below the highest point of the mountain.

Source of the Tawe, the Black Mountain

Drawn & etched by J.G. Wood

1813

CARMARTHENSHIRE 3

CARMARTHEN

OS 159 : 415 203

Carmarthen, delightfully situated on the western bank of the Tywi, is the site of the Roman Caer Maridunum of which the ruined walls were still standing in the 13th century. In c.1096 the Normans established a castle and walled borough here, the former being restored by Edward I in c. 1113 when the town was granted its first charter. In 1403 and 1405 the town and castle were taken by Owain Glyndŵr and by the mid 15th century the first festival using the title 'eisteddfod' was held here. Today there are still remains of the castle to be seen, especially the gatehouse and curtain wall, but much was pulled down first to build a prison and then the present municipal buildings. Other buildings of interest today are the 18th century Guildhall and the Parish Church of St Peter.

Carmarthen

Drawn D. Cox & engraved by W. Radclyffe

1844

CARMARTHENSHIRE 4

DINEFWR PARK & CASTLE

OS 159 : 615 225

Dinefwr Park was created in 18th century by Capability Brown and is now managed by the National Trust. In the park there are the White Park cattle, a breed of cattle that have been associated with Dinefwr for over 900 years. Near the entrance to the Park is Newton House, a 17th century house, which was substantially altered and re-faced with limestone in the 19th century. In 1990 the National Trust carried out a major restoration programme on the house. At the far end of the park, standing proud in a strategic position high above the Tywi Valley is Dinefwr Castle. This has been a fortified site since the Iron Age and a castle may have been built there as early as 877. Soon afterwards it became the court of Hywel Dda, the ruler of much of South West Wales and Gwynedd. The present castle dates back to the early 12th century, when Rhys ap Gruffydd was the ruler of South West Wales. Four miles west of Dinefwr Castle there is another Welsh castle at Dryslyn (OS 159 : 554 204).

Dinefwr Castle

Drawn by J.T. Barber & aquatinted by W. Pickett

c.1803

CARMARTHENSHIRE 5
KIDWELLY CASTLE & CHURCH

OS 159 : 410 071

Virtually nothing now remains of the original 12th century Kidwelly Castle, built on a step rocky height by Roger Bishop of Salisbury. What is seen today dates back to c.1275. The fine Gatehouse is 14th century and is unusual in that it is part of the outer curtain rather than the inner curtain and is also part of the original defences of the town. From the fine castellated towers there are superb views of Carmarthen Bay and the countryside either side of the Towy. Not far from the castle is the Church of St Mary Kidwelly, the successor to a former Benedictine priory founded in 1130 by Roger, Bishop of Salisbury, as a dependency of Sherborne Abbey in Dorset. The present church can be dated back to c.1320, but was heavily restored in 1884 after the spire had been struck by lightning. The church is cruciform and in the gothic style.

Kidwelly Castle

Drawn by J.P. Neale & engraved by Woolnorth

1813

CARMARTHENSHIRE 6

LAUGHARNE & LLANSTEFFAN

OS 159 : 303 107

On either side of the confluence of the River Taff and the River Towy are two important coastal castles. On the bank of the Taff is Laugharne Castle, which consists of two 12-13th century towers and traces of the Tudor mansion of Sir John Perrot. Cadw have beautifully restored the gardens round the castle. Laugharne was also the home of poet Dylan Thomas and his boathouse (NT), where he wrote many of his poems, is open to the public. He is buried in the churchyard of St Martin's Church. On the bank of the Towy is the large ruined Llansteffan Castle, which was built in the 11th-13th century, but is a successor to an earlier defensive earthwork. The main feature of the castle today is the fine gatehouse (c.1280), which seems to have been converted to a keep and living quarters.

Laugharne Castle

Drawn by H. Gastineau & engraved by S. Lacey

1830

CARMARTHENSHIRE 7

LLANDOVERY & LLANDEILO

OS 146 : 770 341

The busy market town of Llandovery is at the junction of three main roads and three rivers. The Welsh translation of Llandovery into English is *'The Church of many waters'* and an old saying states that one cannot leave the Church of St. Dingat without crossing water, which is absolutely true, as the church is surrounded by the rivers Tywi, Bran and Gwydderig. The Romans built a five-acre fort to defend the river and the site of this fort is near the car park. However, the remains of the castle that can be seen today are Norman and were built in the 13th century, and consist of an oval motte, a square bailey and some later masonry. The pleasant town of Llandeilo is set high above the River Tywi and takes its name from St Teilo, who is thought to have founded a monastery here in 560, and the Parish Church is dedicated to his honour.

Llandovery Castle

Drawn & etched by J.G. Wood

1811

CARMARTHENSHIRE 8

LLANDYBIE, GLYNHIR WATERFALL

OS 159 : 642 152

Just off the main road in Llandybie, near the golf course, is the 17th century Glynhir mansion, which was the family home of the DuBuisson family until 1821. Today it is used as bed and breakfast establishment. The River Loughor flows through the estate and in a heavily leafed glade on the edge of the estate can be seen the charming Glynhir Waterfall. As this fall is in private grounds one must ask permission from the mansion to visit it. H. Hughes in 1823 describes is as follows *'The chief beauty of this fall consists in its peculiar position, and the more rare but prominent advantage of being always supplied with a sufficiency of water to give it full beauty.'*

Glynhir Waterfall

Drawn & engraved on wood by H. Hughes

1823

CARMARTHENSHIRE 9

NEWCASTLE EMLYN

OS 145 : 311 407

The new castle of Emlyn lies on a low promontory, skirted on two sides by the River Teifi. The Welsh Prince Maredudd ap Rhys Gryg built the 'New Castle' c.1240 on a site that had very obvious good defensive qualities and provided a good administrative centre. When Maredudd's allied himself to the English forces c.1259, the Welsh lords tried, convicted him of treason and imprisoned him at Criccieth Castle. On Maredudd's death his castles at Emlyn and Dryslwyn passed on to his son Rhys. Eventually the castle passed to the Crown, which marked the start of a new building programme c.1320. In 1645 the castle was finally blown up and made indefensible.

Newcastle Emlyn Castle

Drawn & etched by J.G. Wood

1812

CARMARTHENSHIRE 10

TALLEY ABBEY

OS 146 : 634 328

Talley Abbey was founded in the late 12th century c.1184 by Rhys ap Gruffydd and is the only Premonstratensian Abbey in Wales. The domestic buildings have almost totally disappeared, but though the ruins are scanty they are of considerable interest. The abbey consists of a short presbytery, which is flanked by three chapels on each side. It has a long aisle nave of eight bays west of a central tower. This lay out is much more typical of a Cistercian Abbey than that of a house of White Canons. The today the skeleton of the Abbey's central tower together with parts of the nave, the choir and the transepts, with their chapels, go together to make up the most significant remains of the former abbey. The Abbey was dissolved c.1536.

Talley Abbey

Drawn & etched by J.G. Wood

1813

THE ANCIENT COUNTY OF CARDIGANSHIRE

Cavern Cascade

Drawn by J.W. Smith & Aquatinted by J. Stadler

c.1810

THE ANCIENT COUNTY OF CARDIGANSHIRE

1. Aberaeron

2. Aberystwyth

3. Cardigan

4. Devil's Bridge

5. Hafod

6. Parson's Bridge

7. Llanddewi-Brefi

8. St. David's College, Lampeter

9. Strata Florida Abbey

10. Tregaron

CARDIGANSHIRE 1

ABERAERON

OS 146 : 456 627

The charming harbour at Aberaeron is full of character and well worth a visit. In Alban Square, near the harbour, there are a number of colourful Georgian styled houses, which set off the whole area to great advantage. The harbour was greatly improved by the building of a new pier, at the personal expense of The Revd Alban Gwynne of Tyglyn who, also at his own expense, obtained an act of Parliament for this purpose. Near the seashore are the vestiges of an ancient circular encampment called Castell Cadwgan, which, according to tradition, says was erected by King Cadwgan c.1148.

Aberaeron

Drawn by H. Gastineau & engraved by J. Hinchcliffe

1830

CARDIGANSHIRE 2

ABERYSTWYTH

OS 135 : 583 817

Aberystwyth is the main town on Cardigan Bay and as such is lively seaside resort, the base of the Vale of Rheidol Railway and the home of the National Library of Wales and of the University College of Wales. The first castle at Aberystwyth was built c.1110 and the earth works can still be seen south of the present castle. The new castle dates from 1277 and in 1294 was strong enough to resist a Welsh siege. Owain Glendŵr captured the castle in 1404 and finally it was blown up in 1649. North of the town is Llanbadarn Fawr, which in the 6th century was an important Celtic monastery and bishopric, founded by St Padarn c. 546. The present church (13th–15th century) is one of the largest in Wales and has a mass of interesting artefacts.

Aberystwyth Castle

Drawn & engraved on wood by H. Hughes

1823

CARDIGANSHIRE 3

CARDIGAN

OS 145 : 180 460

The most attractive feature of the county town of Cardigan is the ancient seven arched bridge over the Teifi, which was rebuilt in 1726. Immediately north of the bridge are the ruins of Cardigan Castle. The castle is of Norman origin but it became the most important stronghold of Lord Rhys. In 1171 Lord Rhys rebuilt the defences in stone and mortar, making it the first recorded Welsh castle in stone. Soon after this Cardigan Castle became a pawn in the destructive rivalry between Rhys's heirs Maeglgwn and Gruffudd. Today there are remains of a retaining wall, with turrets on the south and east, built round a derelict mansion, which incorporates part of the original keep. The castle is currently being restored and is on view on some days. Priory Street recalls a medieval Benedictine house that once was here but there are no remains today.

Cardigan Bridge & Castle

Drawn by F. Grose & engraved by J. Grieg

c.1815

CARDIGANSHIRE 4

DEVIL'S BRIDGE

OS 135 : 743 770

There are in fact three bridges, one over the other, spanning the tremendous gorge over the river Mynach, which are collectively called The Devil's Bridge. The top bridge is an iron bridge built in 1901. Below this is a second bridge built in the mid 18th century. In 1814 Thomas Johnes of Hafod added his own iron balustrade to this second bridge. Below this second bridge is the original and ancient stone bridge. It was thought that no one but the devil could construct a piece of masonry in such a situation (hence the name The Devil's Bridge). It is thought that the monks of Strata Florida built this bridge, whose abbey was eight miles away and provided a crossing over the Mynach to their 'hospitium' at Ysbyty Cynfyn.

Devil's Bridge

Wood engraving Drawn & engraved by H. Hughes

1823

CARDIGANSHIRE 5

HAFOD

OS 135 : 759 734

The fame of the Hafod estate was created by Thomas Johnes of Croft Castle, who inherited it from his father in 1780. In 1786 the foundation stone was laid for a new house built by Thomas Baldwin of Bath and further additions, including a new library, were built by Nash. Thomas Johnes also set about creating a number of exciting walks and gardens, which made extensive use of the superb scenery surrounding that part of the Ystwth Valley. Sadly the house and library were burnt in a disastrous fire in 1807 and although they were rebuilt by the time of Thomas Johnes death in 1816, the estate had slowly began to fall into decay. Eventually in the 20th century the house, for safety reasons, was blown up. Today, thanks to the Hafod Trust, the walks have been restored and the public can visit the estate on foot.

Piran Cascade entire, Hafod

Drawn by J.W. Smith & aquatinted by J. Stadler

1810

By kind permission of Llyfrgell Genedlaethol Cymru / The National Library of Wales.

CARDIGANSHIRE 6

PARSON'S BRIDGE

OS 135 : 748 791

Parson's Bridge is situated a few miles east of Devil's Bridge, deep in the Rhiedol Valley, near a hamlet called Ysbyty Cynfyn, which was formally an 'Hospitium' of the monks at Strata Florida (see page 113), The bridge is approached by an easy footpath starting from the side the small church yard. The bridge today is a sturdy narrow bridge placed over the turbulent Rhiedol below. Originally it was a very narrow bridge in order to provide access for the parson to get to his church at Ysbyty Cynfyn. In the 19th century Black's Guide it is described as a bridge *'of just two trees, or rude pieces of timber, laid across a formidable chasm, from rock to rock, with a slight hand-rail on one side only, while below the Rheidol rushes through a narrow channel, forming a whirlpool and roaring with a terrific din.'* It is well worth a visit.

Parson's Bridge

Drawn by J.W. Smith & aquatinted by J. Stadler

1810

By kind permission of Llyfrgell Genedlaethol Cymru / The National Library of Wales.

CARDIGANSHIRE 7

LLANDDEWI BREFI

OS 146 : 664 554

Llanddewi Brefi, as the name suggests, is where St David (Dewi) attended a synod in 519, which was possibly convened to refute the Pelagian heresy, but more likely for the enforcement of local rules and discipline. The Church of St David stands on a mound, which tradition says rose up as David preached. The church can trace its history back for 700 years but the present building was built in 1287 together with a college for clergy. The church was restored in the 19th century after the transepts had collapsed. Inside the church there are a number of ancient stones, one of which is known as St David's staff, others have been damaged and some in the18th or 19th century were sadly used to repair damage in the nave.

Llanddewi Brefi

Drawn & etched by J.G. Wood

1812

CARDIGANSHIRE 8

ST DAVID'S COLLEGE, LAMPETER

OS 146 : 580 480

Lampeter, or Llanbedr Pont Stephan, lies low below wooded hills on the west side of the River Teifi. Near the town there is a fine bridge over the River Teifi that some say was built in the time of King Stephen. An alternative tradition says that a person named Stephen, at his own cost and at a date unknown, built the bridge. The chief place of interest at Lampeter is St David's College, which was built in 1827 by Bishop Burgess of St David's as a theological college for men who hoped to be ordained as ministers of the church, but could not afford the cost of a university education at Cambridge or Oxford. The original college buildings are grouped around a quadrangle and lie within pleasant grounds where there is an ancient motte, and is clearly shown on the engraving below. In 1971 St David's College became a constituent college of the University of Wales.

St. David's College, Lampeter

Drawn by H. Gastineau & engraved by J.C. Varrall

1830

CARDIGANSHIRE 9

STRATA FLORIDA

OS 135 : 746 656

The Cistercian monks were well known for seeking out remote places for their monasteries and Strata Florida Abbey, or Ystrad Fflur, the Vale of Flowers, is no exception. The abbey was founded in the 12th century and grew to become not just an important religious house but also an influential centre of Welsh culture, patronised by princes and poets, many who are believed to have been buried here, including the greatest medieval Welsh poet, Dafydd ap Gwilym. The most striking feature of the abbey ruins today is the beautifully carved west doorway, which frames the green hill sheep farming country, probably established by the monks, who managed many extensive upland estates in mid Wales. Although the abbey today is in ruins the plan of the original church can still be clearly seen. Within the transepts there is a fine collection of medieval floor tiles recovered from the abbey.

Remains of Strata Florida Abbey

Drawn & engraved on wood by H. Hughes

1823

CARDIGANSHIRE 10

TREGARON

OS 146 : 680 597

The small town of Tregaron is situated on the River Berwyn, which joins the Teifi a little lower down and is an important centre for the many sheep farms that surround the town. It owes its name to Caron, a local chieftain and a self-declared bishop of the 2nd–3rd century. To the south east of Tregaron one can follow the remarkably beautiful and barren drovers road to Llanwrtyd Wells, where, about half way along it, there is a diversion to the huge three miles long Llyn Brianne reservoir. To the north of Tregaron is the Cors Caron Nature Reserve, which covers an area of some three square miles of marsh land on either side of the Teifi and is of particular interest to botanists and ornithologists, may of whom keep a special watch for the famous red kites that can be seen in the countryside around Tregaron.

Tregaron

Drawn & etched by J.G. Wood

1812

THE ANCIENT COUNTY OF GLAMORGANSHIRE

Neath Castle

Drawn & etched by J.G. Wood

1813

THE ANCIENT COUNTY OF GLAMORGANSHIRE

1. Aberdulais

2. Caerphilly

3. Cardiff

4. Ewenny Priory & Margam Abbey

5. Castell Coch

6. The Gnoll

7. Merthyr Tydfil

8. Swansea

9. Neath Abbey & Castle

10. Melincourt Waterfall

GLAMORGANSHIRE 1

ABERDULAIS

OS 170 : 772 995

Aberdulais Fall has long been known as a place of natural beauty. It has also seen a succession of industries beginning with copper smelting in 1584, followed by flour and grist mills. It was here that the artist W.W. Young prospered for a time as a miller and corn-factor and he may have leased the Fforest Farm in order to extend the scope of his activities. The industrial remains visible today belonged to a tin-plate works which opened in 1830 and closed about 1890. Today the National Trust owns this beautiful site and has restored the huge water wheel, which draws its water from the top of the fall and generates enough electricity for the whole property.

Aberdulais

Drawn by J. Baker & aquatinted by J. Bluck

c.1795

GLAMORGANSHIRE 2

CAERPHILLY

OS 171 : 157 871

The huge and distinctive castle at Caerphilly covers an area of 30 acres, which makes it the largest castle in Wales. Caerphilly Castle was built in 1268 by the Anglo-Norman lord Gilbert de Clare but was destroyed by Llewelyn in 1270 and then rebuilt and Gilbert de Clare and the Despensers. The castle is a model of the concentric plan adopted by Edward I with its 'walls within walls' system of defence. It also has an elaborate water defence in that it is completely surrounded by a lake as well as an outer and an inner moat, which were all created by the damming the small Nant y Gledr. The castle is approached first by the Great Gatehouse and then by the East Gatehouse into the inner ward, where there are the remains of the drum towers at the corners, (blown up by Cromwell), one of which has a large 50ft segment leaning over from its base by over 11ft, now known as 'the leaning tower'. The castle is in the care of Cadw.

Caerphilly Castle

Drawn by A. Wilson & engraved by Wood

1812

GLAMORGANSHIRE 3

CARDIFF

OS 171 : 180 766

Cardiff, the capital of Wales, is an elegant and progressive city and port, which combine a number of national and county roles with great success. These include the historic Cardiff Castle with its well laid out grounds set in the centre of the city. On the outskirts there is the equally impressive Llandaff Cathedral, combining modern architecture with the old, following bomb damage during the war. Surrounding Cathays Park are the fine early 20th century buildings, which include the Law courts, the City Hall, the National Museum of Wales and the University College. Huge changes have taken place in the area of Cardiff Bay near Penarth. In 2000 the splendid Millennium Stadium was built and is now a centre for international sport and of course the national Welsh rugby team. At St Fagans, just four miles south of central Cardiff is the home of the fantastic Welsh Folk Museum.

The Tower in Cardiff Castle

Published by S. Hooper & engraved by S. Mazell

1775

GLAMORGANSHIRE 4

EWENNY PRIORY & MARGAM ABBEY

OS 170 : 913 778 & 170 : 802 864

Ewenny Priory was founded in 1441 by Maurice de Lundres, as a cell of the great Benedictine abbey of St Peter at Gloucester, and his tomb is in the south transept. The church is now the parish church and is the best example of pure Norman architecture in Wales. The church is in two parts separated by a 13th or 14th rood screen. The nave was used as the parish church and the chancel was the part used by the monks. The remains of the gatehouse and other domestic buildings are incorporated into the priory house on the south.

A few miles away are the remains of Margam Abbey a Cistercian abbey, founded c.1147. The nave is still used today as a church and the rest of the abbey is 13th and 14th century, which includes a fine twelve-sided chapter house with its former central support pillar.

Ewenny Priory

Drawn by H. Gastineau & engraved by H.W. Bond

1830

GLAMORGANSHIRE 5

CASTELL COCH

OS 171 : 132 828

Castell Coch is just like a fairy tale castle with its distinctive conical towers and sharp turrets, which rises romantically out of wooded slopes on which it is built. This castle was the inspiration of the Victorian architect William Burgess who designed and then started to build in 1835 this amazing castle for the 3rd Marquess of Bute, the owner of Cardiff's prosperous docks. Castell Coch has been built on the site of an original 13th century 'Red Castle', so called because it was built in red sandstone. Fragments of this original castle can still be seen at the base of the tower (near the car park) and in the dungeons The castle today is approached by a working portcullis and drawbridge and on entering the castle one is greeted by an amazing interior full of fantastic stone carving, painted ceilings, wallpapers and a whole host of elaborate furniture. Today Castell Coch is in the care of Cadw and attracts masses visitors through its doors.

Red Castle (Castell Coch)

Drawn by J.C. Ibbetson & engraved by J. Bluck (?)

1785

GLAMORGANSHIRE 6

THE GNOLL, NEATH

OS 170 : 765 975

In 1686 The Gnoll became the home of the wealthy industrialist Sir Humphrey Mackworth. The house rose with baronial pomp and grandeur on the brow of a hill, overlooking the town of Neath and the adjacent countryside, giving an impressive appearance in every direction. The grounds were laid out with great sensitivity toward the natural features of the surrounding scenery. This was largely due to the skill of Sir Humphrey Mackworth's son and grandson, both called Herbert who, between the years 1705 and 1740, created the fishponds and cascades. Today only remains of the house and cellars survive; but much of the superb grounds have been carefully restored, including the ponds, cascades and many of its former architectural features. Thanks to the Neath Borough Council these famous eighteenth century grounds are now open to the public most days of the year.

The Gnoll, Neath

Drawn & etched by W.W. Young

1835

GLAMORGANSHIRE 7

MERTHYR TYDFIL

OS 160 : 043 074

Merthyr Tydfil' fame as the former *'iron and steel capital of the world'* began in 1759 when John Guest's Dowlais Ironworks were opened, followed in 1765 by the Crawshay's massive works at Cyfartha and even more foundries in 1767 and in 1784. The extension of the Monmouthshire canal from Merthyr to Cardiff was also a great boost to the industry, as were the tramway in 1802, and Brunel's railway to Cardiff in 1841. By 1831 the population of Merthyr was more than the combined populations of Cardiff, Swansea and Newport! The industrial decline came early in the 20th century, largely due to the importing of cheaper ore from abroad. Merthyr's former industrial prestige is now recalled in the Ynysfach Iron Heritage Centre, housed in a 19th century engine house. An example of the wealth of the powerful ironmasters can be seen at mock gothic Cyfartha Castle, built as the home for the Crawshay family, and now a museum and art gallery.

Cyfartha Iron Works, Merthyr Tydfil

Drawn & etched by J.G. Wood

1811

GLAMORGANSHIRE 8

SWANSEA

OS 159 : 658 931

Swansea is a commercial, residential, academic city, port and the main shopping centre for south west Wales. It sprawls along and above the north-west shore of Swansea Bay, mostly along the right hand bank of the River Tawe, while the docks stretch along the lower left hand bank. By 1700 Swansea was the largest port in Wales, which was greatly increased in 1798 with the construction of the Swansea Canal when tin plate and coal became the principle exports. The city centre was largely reconstructed after air raid damage during the Second World War and is now a modern spacious development. Swansea Castle was built by Norman Henry Beaumont in c.1099, but was later destroyed by Owain Glyndŵr. The most significant remains today are the large square tower, with a remarkable set of light arches surrounding the top, and a few parts of the original castle. Over the years the site of this castle has been used as town hall, a market house, a gaol and as a barracks.

Entrance to Swansea Harbour

Drawn by H. Gastineau & engraved by J. Rogers

1830

GLAMORGANSHIRE 9

NEATH ABBEY & CASTLE

OS 170 : 740 974

Neath Abbey was established in 1130 as a house for Sauvigniac monks, but by 1147 it had become a Cistercian abbey. It quickly achieved prosperity, mainly by trading in wool and hides. However, by the Dissolution (1539) it had declined, supporting only eight monks. In the 16th century, part of the abbey was converted into a mansion for John Herbert, and in the 18th century a part was used for copper smelting. Thus Neath Abbey has had, perhaps the unique distinction, of having served religious, residential and industrial needs. Neath Castle was founded c.1130 as a successor to a motte and bailey, near the abbey buildings. The castle has suffered several disasters. Attacked by the Welsh in 1185, rebuilt, attacked again in 1231 by Llewelyn the Great and again in 1258. It was then destroyed and rebuilt.

Neath Castle, in the center of Neath, was regarded as tenable in 1404, but probably quickly fell into decay fairly soon afterwards. Today little remains other than the outer face of the gateway with two towers linked by an arch.

Neath Abbey

Drawn & etched by W.W. Young

1835

GLAMORGANSHIRE 10

MELINCOURT WATERFALL

OS 170 : 827 017

The Melincourt Waterfall is the anglicized form of Melin-y-Cwrt, the Mill of the Court. This delightful fall of about 80ft is approached through a lush green glen, which makes a refreshing change from its dull industrial surroundings. It was not always so, as in the 18th century, a great ironworks, with an overshot mill, was built near the fall. Remains of this can be seen in the northern boundary of the reserve. This can be clearly seen in a T.Hornor picture with its large overshot water wheel powered by water carried in a channel from above the falls. At the base of the fall, there are many symmetrical rectangular shaped rocks, which have broken off from the top of the fall. Originally, before these fell, one could have walked behind the falls. The Glamorgan Wildlife Trust now manages the whole area around the fall.

Melincourt Waterfall

Drawn by J. Warwick Smith & aquatinted by S. Alken

1794

THE ANCIENT COUNTY OF PEMBROKESHIRE

St David's Cathedral

Drawn by H. Gastineau & engraved by T.H. Shepherd

1830

THE ANCIENT COUNTY OF PEMBROKESHIRE

1. Fishguard

2. Haverfordwest

3. Lamphey Palace

4. Pembroke Castle

5. Pentre Ifan

6. St David's Cathedral

7. St Dogmael's Abbey

8. St Govan's Chapel & Well

9. Solva

10. Tenby

PEMBROKESHIRE 1

FISHGUARD

OS 157 : 955 370

Fishguard is divided into the upper and lower towns. The upper town is a small pleasant town, situated high above the harbour, and contains the main shopping and business area. The picturesque lower town is an extension to the old harbour at the head of the River Gwaun. This was the setting for the 1971 film of Dylan Thomas's 'Under Milk Wood'. The church in the lower town was once a daughter church of St Dogmael's Abbey (see p.138). Between 1894-1906 the new and important Fishguard Harbour was built at Goodwick and is now the base for the regular sea service to Rosslare, in Ireland.

Goodwick Pier, Near Fishguard

Drawn & aquatinted by William Daniell

1814

By kind permission of Llyfrgell Genedlaethol Cymru / The National Library of Wales.

PEMBROKESHIRE 2
HAVERFORDWEST

OS 157 : 947 155

The county town of Pembrokeshire is Haverfordwest, which is dominated by the impressively sited castle. The first castle to be built on this site was built by Gilbert de Clare, in about 1120. However, what one sees today are the remains of a later 13th century castle. This castle had fallen into disuse by 1530. In 1779 a gaol was built within the inner wall and an extension to this was built in 1820, which is now the home of the museum and art gallery. Close to the castle are the remains of a priory church, founded, in about 1207, for Augustinian Canons by Robert Fitz-Tanred. The priory at the Dissolution was largely demolished and left in ruins. However, recently Cadw carried out a major excavation, revealing the extensive foundations of both the priory and its domestic buildings.

Haverfordwest Priory

Drawn by S. Prout & aquatinted by H. Pyall

1829

PEMBROKESHIRE 3

LAMPHREY PALACE

OS 158 : 019 009

The ruins of the Bishop's Palace are set in a quiet valley and flanked by former fishponds. Lamphey Palace was in the main built by Bishop Gower, Bishop of St David's from 1328-1347, but it was not completed until the 16th century under the influence of Bishop Vaughan (1509-22). Lamphey was just one of several manors of the medieval bishops of St David's (eg Llawhaden Castle, Cresswell and St David's). Despite the troubled early medieval period, and in contrast to St David's and Llawhaden, Lamphey has virtually no defensive features and the bishops lived there in considerable elegance and comfort until 1549, when it passed to the Crown.

Lamphey Palace

Drawn by H. Gastineau & engraved by H. Bond

1830

PEMBROKESHIRE 4

PEMBROKE

OS 157 : 983 015

Pembroke's main attraction is its fine castle, which was built shortly after the Norman Conquest by Roger Montgomery in the late 11th century. William Marshall, who became the first Earl of Pembroke, rebuilt the castle between 1189 and 1245, which included the Great Tower, the Norman Hall and inner defences. In 1454 the Castle and Earldom were passed on to Jasper Tudor whose nephew, the future King Henry VII, was born at Pembroke Castle. During the Civil war Cromwell sacked Pembroke Castle when the town's military governor changed his allegiance from the Parliamentarians to the Royalists. After many centuries of lying derelict the castle has been well restored over the last 120 years and is now a major tourist attraction.

Pembroke Castle

Drawn & aquatinted by P. Sandby

1775

By kind permission of Llyfrgell Genedlaethol Cymru / The National Library of Wales.

PEMBROKESHIRE 5

PENTRE IFAN

OS 145 : 959 370

The Burial chamber of Pentre Ifan is set in a remote site on rocky moorland. It is not far from Carn Ingli, with its Iron Age fort and settlement, once the home of St Brynach, the patron saint of the church at Nevern. Pentre Ifan is an impressive communal burial chamber, whose origins can be traced back to at least 2000BC. Pentre Ifan, inspite of its great antiquity, it is still remarkably well preserved and consists of a long capstone supported by massive uprights. Just south of Pentre Ifan are the Preseli Hills, with their famous bluestones, thought to be the source of the massive stones at Stonehenge.

Pentre Ifan, Near Nevern

Drawn by Richard C. Hoare & engraved by J. Grieg

1810

By kind permission of Llyfrgell Genedlaethol Cymru / The National Library of Wales.

PEMBROKESHIRE 6

ST. DAVID'S

OS 157 : 751 254

The cathedral church of St David's owes its origins to St David who was born at St Nons's in 530 AD. The present cathedral dates from the 12th century and was built by a Florentine monk, Bishop Peter de Leia. Since that time the cathedral has suffered not only in war but also as a result of fire and earth tremors, which may account for the leaning pillars in the nave. Considerable restoration work was carried out in the 18th century, when John Nash rebuilt the west front and further work in the 19th century by Sir Gilbert Scott. The interior of St David's Cathedral is 298ft long, 68ft wide between the nave and aisles and 131ft wide between the transepts. The curious sloping nave has six, well carved late Norman bays with a clerestory and triforium. The splendid flat roof is of Irish oak and was probably erected the years 1472 and 1509. The fine Rood Screen is the work of Bishop Gower (1328-47).

St David's Cathedral

Drawn and engraved on wood by H. Hughes

1823

PEMBROKESHIRE 7

ST. DOGMAEL'S ABBEY

OS 145 : 164 458

St Dogmael's Abbey was one of the very few a Tironensian abbeys in Britain and was founded c.1113-15 by Robert Martyn, Lord of the Cemaes area. It was a daughter house of the reformed Benedictine order from Tiron in Normandy and eventually became a Benedictine Abbey in its own right in 1120. Its nucleus was the church at Llandudoch, which adjoins the abbey, but in a rebuilt form. This church was built on an earlier monastery destroyed by the Vikings in 987. In 2008 a new visitor centre has been built at St Dogmael's Abbey, which now houses a collection of 5th and 6th century carved Christian stones.

St. Dogmael's Priory

Drawn & aquatinted by H. Hassell

1806

PEMBROKESHIRE 8

ST. GOVAN'S CHAPEL & WELL

OS 158 : 967 929

The small Chapel of St Govan, sited at the foot of a steep climb towards the sea, is simply furnished with stone altar and benches, dating back at least to the 13th century and possibly to the 6th century. St Govan was a 6th century Irishman from Wexford. In his old age St Govan came to Pembroke in order to find a suitable place to live out the life of a hermit. Tradition has it that he miraculously found the site where he built his chapel and continued to live there until he died in 586. Below St Govan's Chapel, among the limestone rocks, is St Govan's Well. This well is now empty, but in former times its water were said to have had healing properties, particularly in the of cure eye troubles. It also presumably provided fresh water to the hermits and pilgrims who came to visit St Govan's Chapel.

St Govan's Chapel

Drawn by H. Gastineau & engraved by H. Jorden

1830

PEMBROKESHIRE 9

SOLVA

OS 157 : 805 243

Solva, or Lower Solva, as it should be known, was until the 19th century a reasonably important fishing harbour, as is shown in the engraving below. Today it has become a picturesque tourist attraction at the head of a long and narrow creek, which, at high tide together with the huge number of colourful sailing boats, presents a charming photographic picture. On The Gribin, the headland to the south of the harbour, one can see the remains of Iron Age earthworks. It also provides a superb view of the coast and, to the south, of the first lighthouse for 'The Smalls', which was built in 1773 and shipped out from Solva to the rocks on 'The Smalls' 16 miles west of Skomer Island.

Solva, near St. David's

Drawn & aquatinted by William Daniell

1814

By kind permission of Llyfrgell Genedlaethol Cymru / The National Library of Wales.

PEMBROKESHIRE 10

TENBY

OS 158 : 132 004

Tenby, although a very popular holiday resort, still retains a certain amount of its Victorian charm. It is a walled town that has much that is of historical interest. One enters the town by a fine medieval gateway (originally there were five). The town walls were repaired in 1457 and again in 1588 at the time of the Spanish Armada. South Gate is protected by a semicircular barbican, which retains its original entrance on the north side. St Mary's church is particularly interesting as it contains features of practically every age since the 13th century. There are remains of the 13th century Tenby Castle on Castle Hill, which on the north side leads down to the harbour. In the town one can visit the Tudor Merchants' House (NT) on Quay Hill, a fine example of a wealthy merchant's home during the late 15th century.

A Panoramic View of Tenby

A coloured lithograph by G.P. Reinagle

1832

By kind permission of Llyfrgell Genedlaethol Cymru / The National Library of Wales.

THE ANCIENT COUNTY OF RADNORSHIRE

Old Radnor

Drawn by H. Gastineau & engraved by J. Hinchcliffe

1830

Old Radnor was originally the county town of Radnorshire. This was then transferred to New Radnor (see p.151) and finally this was transferred to Llandrindod Wells(see p.150), now the county town of Powys.

THE ANCIENT COUNTY OF RADNORSHIRE

1. Aberedw

2. Cwmhir Abbey

3. Elan Vale

4. Knighton

5. Llandrindod Wells

6. New Radnor

7. Penkerrig

8. Presteigne

9. Rhayader

10. Water-Break-Its-Neck

RADNORSHIRE 1

ABEREDW

OS 147 : 080 474

The charming hamlet of Aberedw is sited at the confluence of the Edw and the Wye and is one of the most enchanting spots in the county of Radnorshire. The Edw descends through a deep valley, but about half a mile before it reaches the Wye it flows through a very narrow rocky channel with tremendous force. This can be quite spectacular when the river is in spate. Close by is the site of Aberedw Castle, which has virtually no remains but is particularly remembered as a favourite retreat of Llewelyn ap Gruffydd. Tradition states that Llewelyn hid in a cave, concealed in the hills south east of the church and now known as Llewelyn's Cave, on the night before he was captured and later put to death by execution at Cimery, near Builth Wells.

Aberedw Castle

Drawn & engraved on wood by H. Hughes

1823

RADNORSHIRE 2
CWMHIR ABBEY

OS 147 : 056 711

Cwmhir Abbey is set in a beautiful pastoral setting in the winding valley of the Clwedog. The abbey was founded in 1143 for Cistercian monks from Whitland, and a second foundation followed in 1176. It was also destroyed twice, first by Henry III in 1231 and again in 1401 by Owain Glyndŵr who thought that the monks were Englishmen in disguise! Although after Henry III's attack an ambitious plan for rebuilding was envisaged, in fact the choir was never built, the transepts were left unfinished and Owain Glyndŵr eventually destroyed the nave. By the time of the Dissolution in 1536 there were only three monks in residence. There are only a few remains of the abbey today but it boasts that the body of Llewelyn Ap Gruffydd was brought here to be buried after his execution in 1282 Some of the former beautiful arcading from the abbey can now be seen in Llanidloes Parish Church.

Abbey Cwm-Hir

Drawn & lithographed by J.M. Ince

1832

By kind permission of Llyfrgell Genedlaethol Cymru / The National Library of Wales.

RADNORSHIRE 3

ELAN VALLEY

OS 147 : 935 655

The Elan Valley Reservoir was built between 1892-1896 and the Claerwen Reservoir was built in 1952, both supplying water to the people of Birmingham. The Elan Reservoir is made up of a chain of five narrow lakes each with a dam and extends some nine miles from North to South. The flooding of the valley provided the theme for the novel 'The House under the Water' by Francis Brett Young. The Claerwen Reservoir, with its impressive 1166ft long dam, runs more or less from east to west and is nearly four miles long and fills its own valley. Roads skirt the entire length of both reservoirs and there are a number of parking places allowing visitors to explore some of the superb countryside, which surrounds the valley. There is also a good visitor's centre where the story of the construction of the reservoirs is explained and refreshments can be purchased. (The engraving below of course was engraved before the dams were constructed.)

Craggs Vale, near the River Elan, Rhayader

Copperplate line engraving by W. Turner

1792

By kind permission of the National Museum of Wales

RADNORSHIRE 4

KNIGHTON

OS 148 : 288 725

Knighton today is a quiet border town situated in a pleasant valley on the southern banks of the small River Teme. However, it had a more turbulent past and this is still recalled today in that the town has two mottes. The first of these mottes is mentioned as far back as 1181 and is at the top of the town, and the second, called Bryn y Castell, is in the valley near the station. Offa's Dyke, which stretches from the coast near Prestatyn in North Wales to Chepstow in South Wales and acted as a dividing line between Wales and England, crosses the south west of Knighton and explains the Welsh name of name of the town, Tref y Clawd, The Town on the Dyke. The Offa's Dyke Heritage Centre is housed in the Old School in the town. On Bryn Glas, a little south of Knighton, a fierce battle was fought between Sir Edward Mortimer and Owain Glyndŵr, in which Sir Edward was defeated with great loss.

Knighton

Drawn & lithographed by J.M. Ince

1832

By kind permission of the National Museum of Wales

RADNORSHIRE 5

LLANDRINDOD WELLS

OS 147 : 057 611

During the mid 18th century the 'healing qualities' of the local springs at Llandrinod attracted many visitors to the area, which resulted in a great economic boom for the town and the building of a grand hotel at Llandrindod Hall. With the discovery of the springs the title of Wells was added to the name of the town making it a popular spa town with its splendid pump rooms at the Rock Park and the Pump House Hotel. This initial boom of prosperity began to decline in the late 18th and early 19th centuries, however this was reversed with the coming of the railway to Llandrindod Wells, making the spa accessible from the Midlands, the North West of England and South Wales. Sadly this prosperity only continued until the First World War, the depressions of the 1920s and 1930s and the closure in the 1960s of the Mid-Wales railway line to Cardiff and North and West Wales. Llandrindod Wells was the capital town of Radnorshire and in 1974 it became the capital of the newly formed administrative county of Powys.

The Arcade, Pump Room & Chalebeate Spring

Vignette line engraving by J Newman & Co.

1880

By kind permission of Llyfrgell Genedlaethol Cymru / The National Library of Wales.

RADNORSHIRE 6

NEW RADNOR

OS 148 : 211 609

New Radnor was once the county town with a castle, walls and gates, but today is just a large village in which the most interesting feature is the large motte and bailey near the church and on which was once an 11th century castle. This castle was later destroyed by King John, rebuilt by Henry III and finally ruined by Owain Glyndŵr in 1401. Historically the castle was the starting point in 1188 of Archbishop Baldwin's tour through Wales with Geraldus to preach the Third Crusade. In the 13th century the town was laid out to the Edwardian plan of square blocks, but of this plan virtually nothing now survives, except that just outside the south west of the town something can be seen of the protective boundary earth work. On the right of the main road from Kington there is an elaborate monument known as 'The Lewis Memorial Cross' erected in 1863 to the memory of Sir George Cornewall Lewis of Harpton Court.

New Radnor

Drawn by J.P. Neale & engraved by W. Smith

c.1815

RADNORSHIRE 7

PENCERRIG

OS 147 : 043 539

The tiny hamlet of Pencerrig, situated just off the main A483 about three miles north of Builth Wells, is particularly remembered for being the home of the landscape artist Thomas Jones (1742-1803). Thomas Jones was intended by his parents to be ordained and was educated at Jesus College, Oxford, but he left Oxford in 1761 in order pursue a career as a painter. He went to London to train under Shipley at the Royal Academy, and finally with the distinguished painter Richard Wilson. His career progressed successfully for the next ten years during which time he painted many landscapes views including several in and around Pencerrig. The engraving below is a coloured aquatint by J. Bluck, after an original drawing by Thomas Jones and is a charming view of a scene near Pencerrig, which was reproduced in the book 'A picturesque guide through Wales' by J. Baker (1794-97).

Scene at Pencerrig

Drawn by T. Jones & aquatinted J. Bluck

1795

By kind permission of Llyfrgell Genedlaethol Cymru / The National Library of Wales.

RADNORSHIRE 8

PRESTEIGNE

OS 148 : 316 646

Presteigne, or Llan Andras, or St Andrew to whom the parish church is dedicated, is an attractive old border town with some good half-timbered houses. The most notable building is 'The Radnorshire Arms', once the home of John Bradshaw (1602-59), whose signature headed those on the death warrant of Charles I. The stone bridge over the River Lugg dates from the 17th century and connects Radnorshire with Herefordshire. The parish church is 14th-16th century, but has fragments of an earlier building, part of the choir arch is pre Norman and there are early Norman remains in the window of the north aisle. In the chapel window there is a mosaic made up of old medieval glass. The low hill west of the town, which is known as 'The Warden', is now a public park but originally was the site of a Norman Castle destroyed by Llewelyn the Last in 1261.

Presteigne

Drawn & lithographed by J.M. Ince

1832

By kind permission of the National Museum of Wales

RADNORSHIRE 9

RHAYADER

OS 147 : 968 678

In the heart of the beautiful Wye Valley is the market town of Rhayader or in Welsh Rhaeadr Gwy (the Waterfall of the Wye). The waterfall below the bridge has virtually gone and this is due the fact that in 1780 a new bridge was built over the Wye and this involved removing much of the rock, over which the Wye flowed in an impressive cataract. Above the river and near to the church, on a steep rocky plateau above the river, can be seen the site of a former castle. Lord Rhys Gruffydd built this castle in 1177, during a power struggle for mid Wales. It was rebuilt in 1194 only to be destroyed by the neighbouring Welsh lords. Tradition states that there was once a monastery for Dominican friars near the bridge. If this is true it was probably no more than a cell of the monks at Strata Florida and there are no remains of it today. The parish church was rebuilt in the early 18th century and later restored in the early English style.

Rhayader Bridge

Drawn by D. Cox & engraved by W. Radclyffe

1844

RADNORSHIRE 10

WATER-BREAK-ITS-NECK WATERFALL

OS 148 : 185 601

Near the village of Llanfihangel nant Melan, just off the A44, there is a track, which leads into the woods where there is a charming waterfall with the curious name of 'Water Break its Neck'. The fall is fed by a small tributary of the Summergil Brook and produces a drop of about 80ft down a hard rock intrusion into a natural amphitheatre, overhung with heavily lichened trees and ferns. The stream falls more or less vertically down the face of the cliff and the surrounds are strewn with the trunks of fallen trees. When the brook is in spate the fall can be quite dramatic but the approach is more difficult. However, even with a small amount of water the idyllic situation and its charming surroundings make the walk well worthwhile. On the approach to the fall one enters 'The Warren Woodland' where there are some very fine trees including the giant Wellingtonia, which can grow to over a 150ft.

Water-Break-Its-Neck

Drawn & lithographed by J.M. Ince

1832

THE ANCIENT COUNTY OF MONMOUTHSHIRE

Tintern Abbey

Drawn by P.J. de Loutherbourg & aquatinted by W. Pickett

1805

THE ANCIENT COUNTY OF MONMOUTHSHIRE

1. Monmouth

2. Blaenavon

3. Caerleon

4. Chepstow

5. Llanthony Priory

6. Abergavenny

7. Tintern Abbey

8. Raglan Castle &Border Castles

9. Newport

10. Usk

MONMOUTHSHIRE 1

MONMOUTH

OS 162 : 509 129

The attractive Border town of Monmouth is situated between the River Wye and The River Monnow, and from the north is entered by the distinctive 13th century gateway over the Monnow, which was built in 1262 and is a rare example in Britain of a fortified gateway on a bridge. Monmouth, in common with many of the Border towns, had its castle, but little of this remains today beyond a 12th century keep, destroyed in 1646. Monmouth used to have a Benedictine priory built by Withenol de Monmouth in the reign of Henry I and dissolved in 1150. The present parish church of St Mary was rebuilt in 1881, though the tower and the spire are older. Inside the church there is a cresset stone c.1102, which is more or less contemporary with the former Priory. Near the church is a building which tradition asserts was once the library of Geoffrey of Monmouth, the historian and perhaps a monk at the priory.

Gateway & Bridge, Monmouth

Drawn by H. Gastineau Engraved by W. Deeble

c. 1805

MONMOUTHSHIRE 2

BLAENAVON

OS 161 : 238 089

North-west of the once famous iron and tin plate industrial town of Pontypool is the former industrial town at Blaenavon, renown for its ironworks and for its colliery. The iron works were a milestone in the history of the Industrial Revolution, for they were the first purpose-built multi-furnace ironworks in Wales, and were established here in 1788-89. By 1796 Blaenavon was the second largest ironworks in Wales producing 5,400 tons of iron a year. These furnaces were eventually closed in 1904, but one can still view much of the works site, including its impressive water balance tower. The colliery was closed in 1980. However, it has since been reopened to the public as the Big Pit Mining Museum where one can view the former coal mining industry both above ground and 300ft underground. Blaenavon's historic iron and coal mining history was recognized in 2000 when the town was declared an UNESCO World Heritage Site.

Iron Works at Blaenavon

Drawn by Sir Richard Hoare & engraved by W. Byrne

1800

By kind permission of Llyfrgell Genedlaethol Cymru / The National Library of Wales.

MONMOUTHSHIRE 3

CAERLEON

OS 171 : 335 902

Caerleon is famous for its Roman past with its Amphitheatre, Barracks, Baths and Legionary Museum. The Fortress dates from c.75 and was known as Castra Legionis, hence Caerleon of today. A legion's normal strength was between 5000-6000 men, and was protected first by earthworks and timber then c.100 by strong walls of stone. The Amphiheatre c.80-100 seated 6000 people and had eight entrances. The Barracks had 64 blocks, originally these were wood and then in the 2nd century the too were replaced by stone. The Baths were discovered in 1964 and are now considered to be the best examples of their kind in Britain, consisting of a huge stone complex (50ft high) with three baths (cold, warm and hot). All this past Roman history is now well illustrated and explained in the excellent Legionary Museum built in 1987 replacing the one built in 1850.

Caerleon, near Newport

Drawn H. Gastineau & engraved by J. Outhwaite

1830

MONMOUTHSHIRE 4

CHEPSTOW

OS 162 : 532 942

Chepstow is an ancient walled border town on the west bank of the River Wye, two miles above where it flows into the River Severn. The town today is noted for its superb Norman castle built by William Fitz Osbern. The castle consists of three wards, a keep and a barbican, which has been built dramatically on the high and steep rocks above the Wye. The entrance to the castle is via the Gatehouse (1225-1245) leading into the lower ward, and on to Marten's Tower (13th century) and then to the Great Tower of which the lower stories are part of the original castle (1067-72). The 13th century Port Wall, which enclosed the medieval town and port, can still be followed along much of the course. However, the present West Gate (1524) replaced an original 13th century gate. The parish church of St Mary has been built over the site of a former Benedictine Priory, also built by William Fitz Osbern c.1072, but the remains of the priory in the church are very slight.

Chepstow Castle & Bridge over the Wye

Drawn H. Warren & engraved by W. Radclyffe

1844

MONMOUTHSHIRE 5

LLANTHONY PRIORY

OS 161 : 288 279

The founders of the great monastic communities had the remarkable knack of discovering the most peaceful and beautiful places for the building of their monasteries, and Llanthony Priory was no exception to this principle. William de Lacey settled there and established a small monastic community in 1108. The small parish church, dedicated to St. David, is thought to stand on the site of this first community church. Llanthony Priory of Augustinian Canons was built between 1180 and 1230 and became one of the great medieval buildings of Wales. The priory was then devastated by Owain Glyndŵr in 1399 causing it to become almost abandoned for fifty years, the majority of the canons going to a new foundation in Gloucester, called Llanthony Secunda. The ruins of the church and priory that survive today date back to the early thirteenth century and part of the priory buildings have been converted into a hotel.

Llanthony Abbey

Lithograph, artist & engraver not known

c.1830

MONMOUTHSHIRE 6

ABERGAVENNY

OS 161 : 301 141

As well as being a busy tourist and shopping centre Abergavenny also has two buildings of special historical interest. The first of these are the remains of Abergavenny Castle, which consists of two towers, one round and the other polygonal, and a gate with a substantial barbican. The traditional motte and bailey were founded in the eleventh century, but the principal ruins belong to the thirteenth and fourteenth centuries. In later centuries this castle has had various additions made to it, including a hunting lodge, now housing an excellent local museum. St. Mary's Priory, now the parish church, was originally a Benedictine priory and a cell of the abbey at Le Mans in France. The church and the castle were both founded by Hameline de Balum (1085-1138).

Abergavenny Church

Drawn & engraved by J. Cullum

c. 1800

MONMOUTHSHIRE 7

TINTERN ABBEY

OS 162 : 535 000

Tintern Abbey was once the wealthiest of the Welsh medieval monasteries and is the best-preserved abbey in Wales. The abbey owes its still rural setting to the Cistercians monks, whose austere rule demanded that their abbeys be in remote places. Its grandeur is due largely to the generosity of Roger Bigod of Chepstow Castle, who financed the rebuilding of the abbey in the late 13th century. It is an outstanding example of the elaborate decorated style of Gothic architecture, providing inspiration for both the artist Turner and the poet Wordsworth. Walter de Clare in 1131 founded the first abbey, the monks coming directly from Normandy. Little of this first abbey remains to day and what one sees today are the 13th century church, the 14th century abbot's quarters and the 15th century infirmary. At the Dissolution in 1536 the lead was stripped off and used at Chepstow and Raglan castles.

Tintern Abbey looking West

Steel vignette engraving, published by Rock & Co

1861

MONMOUTHSHIRE 8

RAGLAN & BORDER CASTLES

OS 161 : 411 084

The border castle at Raglan (Cadw) is a stark and impressive ruin on the top of a knoll and combines defensive requirements with later manorial elegance and comfort. The original motte, on which the Great tower now stands, was raised by William Fitz Osbern c.1067-71; and the present castle was begun by William ap Thomas c. 1430-45 and his son, the Earl of Pembroke, then completed the greater part of the present buildings. Later the property passed on to the Earls of Worcester, who between 1548-89 enlarged the domestic building in a more practical and comfortable style. The castle was defeated in the Civil War c.1646. Today the ruins of the castle have been remarkably well preserved and one can still get a realistic picture of its former glory. While at Raglan Castle it is well worthwhile visiting the Border Castles of White Castle (OS 161 : 378 177). Skenfrith Castle (OS 161 : 458 203) and Grosmont Castle (OS 161 : 405 247).

Raglan Castle

Drawn by J.T. Barber & aquatinted by J. Bluck

1803

MONMOUTHSHIRE 9

NEWPORT

OS 171 : 309 876

Newport is now the Cathedral city of the Diocese of Monmouth, created in 1921, with St Woolos Church being chosen as the cathedral church. Tradition states that St Woolos built the first church on this site in the 6th century. It was rebuilt in 1171 and again in the 15th century. Finally in the 1960s it was extended once it had become a cathedral. The St Mary's Chapel is the most likely site of the original church. The stone castle built in 1191 on the banks of the River Usk, was rebuilt in the 14th century, burnt by Owain Glyndŵr and then much modified in the 15th century. What remains today is the east side of a former ward and a square central tower with two octagonal towers with square bases. Newport boasts in having one of the four known transporter bridges It was built in 1906 and has a movable platform which is capable of carrying loads of up to 120 tons and is still in use today.

St Woolos Church, Newport

Drawn by C.J. Greenwood & lithographed by W. Spreat

c. 1845

By kind permission of the Newport Museum & Art Gallery

MONMOUTHSHIRE 10

USK

OS 171 : 379 008

The small market town of Usk, as its name suggests, is situated on the east bank of the River Usk and is in part spread over the Roman town of Burrium, the predecessor of Caerleon (see p.160). Usk Castle (private) was built in the 12th century and belonged to the De Clares and the Earls of March and was eventually captured by Simon de Montfort in 1265. The remains today include the keep (12th & 15th C) a round tower on the curtain (13th C) and a gatehouse.

The fine parish church was once a Benedictine Nunnery founded in 1236. However the remains of the Norman abbey are few except that the arches of the crossing, the choir and the tower can be dated back to the first half of the 12th century. The priory gatehouse, situated by the churchyard gate, is a survivor of the priory, which was dissolved at the Dissolution.

Porch of Usk Priory

Drawn R. Hoare & engraved by W. Byrne

1800

By kind permission of Llyfrgell Genedlaethol Cymru / The National Library of Wales.

POSTSCRIPT

The putting together of this compendium of ten views for each of the thirteen ancient counties of Wales has proved a much harder task than that which I had when I first conceived the idea of producing such a book.

The problem has been of what views to include and what to omit. This has been made even harder in that for some of the selected views there are masses of images to choose from, whereas others have proved hard to find any images at all.

However, the research that I have undertaken in order to put this book together has greatly increased my appreciation of the many 18th and 19th century books of views, from which I have chosen the prints reproduced in the book.

But what is more important is that I have had enormous pleasure in actually visiting the 130 views themselves and then comparing the prints with the sites as they are today. This in turn has helped me to put together a short description for this book for each of the sites.

My hope is that any who may come across this book will be encouraged to visit the superb sites for themselves and discover something of *'The Beauties of the ancient counties of Wales'*.

David S.Yerburgh

2008

BIBLIOGRAPHY

Views in Wales in Aquatinta. P.W. Sandby	1775
A Tour through Monmouthshire and Wales. H.P. Wyndam	1781
Picturesque Guide through Wales. J. Baker	1791-95
A Tour through parts of North & South Wales. W. Sotheby	1794
A Tour throughout South Wales. J.T. Barber	1803
The Scenery of South Wales. B.H. Malkin	1804
Romantic & Picturesque Scenery. P.J. Loutherbourg	1805
Six Welsh Views. Miss M. Smirke	c.1808
Tour to Hafod. J.E. Smith	1810
The Beauties of Monmouthshire. J. Evans	1810
The Beauties of North Wales. Rev. J. Evans	1812
Principal Rivers of Wales. J.G. Wood	1813
Voyage round Great Britain. W. Daniell	1814-25
The Beauties of South Wales. T. Rees	1815
Cambria Depicta. E. Pugh	1816
The Northern Cambrian Mountains. T. Compton	1817
Sketches in Wales. Artist not known.	1819
A Picturesque Description of North Wales. Pub T. M'Lean	1823
Beauties of Cambria. H. Hughes	1823
Welsh scenery. Captain Batty	1823
Wales Illustrated. Jones & Co.	1830
Views of Tenby. G.P. Reinagle	1832
Seven Views Illustrating the County of Radnor. J.M. Ince	1832
The Beauties of Glyn Neath. W.W. Young	1835
The Cambrian Mountains. T. Compton	1851
Wanderings in North Wales. T. Roscoe	1835
Wanderings in South Wales. T. Roscoe	1844
Black's Guide to South Wales.	1874
Black's Guide to North Wales.	1886
Thorough Guide to South Wales.	1901
Waterfalls of Wales. J.L. Jones	1986
Blue Guide, Wales.	1995
The CADW Guides to their sites in Wales.	1995

LIST OF ARTISTS & ENGRAVERS INCLUDED IN THIS BOOK

Artists
Alstone. M.
Baker. J.
Barber. J.T.
Batty. Capt.
Buck. S.&.N.
Compton. T.
Cox. D.
Cullum. J.
Daniell. W.
Evans.
Fielding. T.H.
Gastineau. H
Griffith. M.
Greenwood.C.J.
Grose. T & F
Hassell. H.
Hillier. G.
Hoare. R.C.
Hooper.S
Hughes. H.
Ibbbetson. J.C.
Ince. J.M.
Ingleby. J.
Laporte. J.
T.Jones
Loutherbourg. P.J.de.
Mudge.
Neale. J.P.
Nicholson. T.
Prout. S.
Pugh. E.
Reinagle. G.P.
Roy. General
Sandby. P.
Samuel. G.
Smirke. M.
Smith. J.'W'.
Sunderland. T.
Turner. J.M.W.
Warren.H.
Wilson.A

Artists
Wood. J.G.
Wrightson. J.
Young. W.W.

Engravers
Adlard. H.
Alken. S.
Baily. J.
Barber. T
Batenham. W.
Bluck. J.
Bond. H. & W.
Buck. S & N
Byrne. R.
Caldwell. J.
Cartwright. T.
Catherall. T.
Compte.
Cullum. J.
Daniell. W.
Deeble. W.
Day. W.
Fielding. T.
Finden. E.
Grieg. J.
Harriden. J.
Hassell.H.
Havell. D.
Havell. J.
Hay.
Hinchcliffe. J.
Hughes. H.
Ince. J.M.
Jorden. H.
Lacey. S.
Matthews.
Mazell. S.
Medland.
Neale. J.P.
Noyce. E.
Newman & Co

Engravers
Outhwaite. J.
Pickett. W.
Poole. W.
Pyall. H.
Ratclyffe. W.
Reinagle. G.P.
Rogers. J.
Sandby. P.
Shepherd. T.H.
Smith. W.
Sparrow.J.
Stadler. J.
Storer. J.
Varrell. J.C.
Wallis. W.
Watts. W.
White.
Whittaker. G.&.B.
Wood
Wood. J.G.
Woolnorth
Young. W.

INDEX

INDEX CONTINUED

INDEX CONTINUED

INDEX

INDEX CONTINUED

ACKNOWLEDGEMENTS

The National Library of Wales, Aberystwyth, especially Paul Joyner, Mike Francis, Lorna Jones, and Sion Jobbins. Also for their kind permission to reproduce many of the images in the NLW collection.

The National Museum of Wales, Cardiff, especially John Kenyon, Beth McIntyre, Charlotte Topsfield and Kay Kays. Also for their kind permission to reproduce many of the images in the NMW collection.

Cadw, Welsh Historical Monuments, especially the late Richard Avent, Peter Humphries and Christine Kenyon, and for the many excellent Cadw publications.

The Royal Commission on the Ancient and Historical Monuments of Wales, especially Penny Icke, for her help over the castles built by the Welsh princes.

The British Museum, for the Turner picture on p.28.

Peter Yerburgh, for his patience and his helpful computer skills.

Ronald Broadbent, for his advice on Welsh Castles and Abbeys.

Marlene Lucas who photographed many of the images from my books of Welsh views.

The 'Blue Guide of Wales' by John Tomes as an invaluable source of information for the various places I selected for this book.

Diana Coleridge for her encouragement throughout the production of my books and her daughter, Rebecca, who was the original inspiration behind the design of the covers for my books.

Idris Davies, for the drawing on p.98.